Exercise Tiger

EXERCISE TIGER

Casualty cover up revealed

Richard T Bass

MENIN HOUSE

Also by Richard T. Bass

Spirits of the Sand (1992)
Precious Cargo (1993)
The Brigades of Neptune (1994)
Clear the Way (1996)
Spirits of the Sand – field edition (2005)
Exercise Tiger (2012)

For more information please visit www.exercise-tiger.com

Menin House an imprint of
Tommies Guides Military Booksellers & Publishers

Gemini House
136-140 Old Shoreham Road
Brighton
BN3 7BD

www.tommiesguides.co.uk

First published in Great Britain by
Tommies Guides, 2017

A catalogue record for this book is available from the British Library

ISBN 978-1-9998900-3-2

Cover design by Ryan Gearing

Printed and bound in Great Britain

Contents

Background 7
Casualty numbers 10
Prepare to move 12
Loading. 15
H-Hour delayed. 18
The run-in 20
Hitting the beach. 22
Mass burials 27
Tip off. 30
E-Boat attack 36
First reports 41
Origins of "749" 45
Official casualty numbers 50
Dates of death. 52
Casualty transport. 53
Burial at Brookwood 60
Blameworthy 63
Cover up 67
Cover-up uncovered 69
Deception 74
Exhumation 77
To Europe 80
Normandy burials 84
Emergency cemeteries 87
Morning Reports 90
Other casualty sources 93
Burial reports:. 94
Remembrance 99
Conclusion 100
Epilogue:. 102

Background

D-DAY, 6th June 1944 was the greatest amphibious operation in military history when north-west Europe was invaded over the beaches of Normandy by American, British and Canadian forces.

For months, American units designated to be within the first waves to hit the beaches had been constantly practising their individual skills in small scale, local exercises ever since their arrival in England. They were all aware of the imminent invasion of Europe and guessed they were to be part of the grand plan but were quite unaware how they would fit in or indeed if they were to be used at all.

Indications as to which units were to spearhead this massive operation became apparent between September 1943 and April 1944 when over 14,000 men of selected Infantry Regiments, Combat Engineers, Rangers, Tank and Artillery battalions were gradually despatched to the U.S. Assault Training Center in North Devon.

Each unit attended an intensive three week course designed around their speciality, concentrating upon co-operation and interaction with other units and the U.S. Navy in amphibious operations. Upon completion of their individual course and returning to station, these newly acquired skills and tactics were rehearsed in more local exercises which now had a positive direction and a strong hint they were to be used in the first waves of invasion.

By early 1944 detailed plans for the Normandy beach assaults were finalised and it was necessary to test their viability in large scale rehearsals. The British and Canadians tested their invasion plans at various locations in Norfolk and along the south coast of England while the Americans had their own requisitioned battle area inland of Slapton Sands in south Devon.

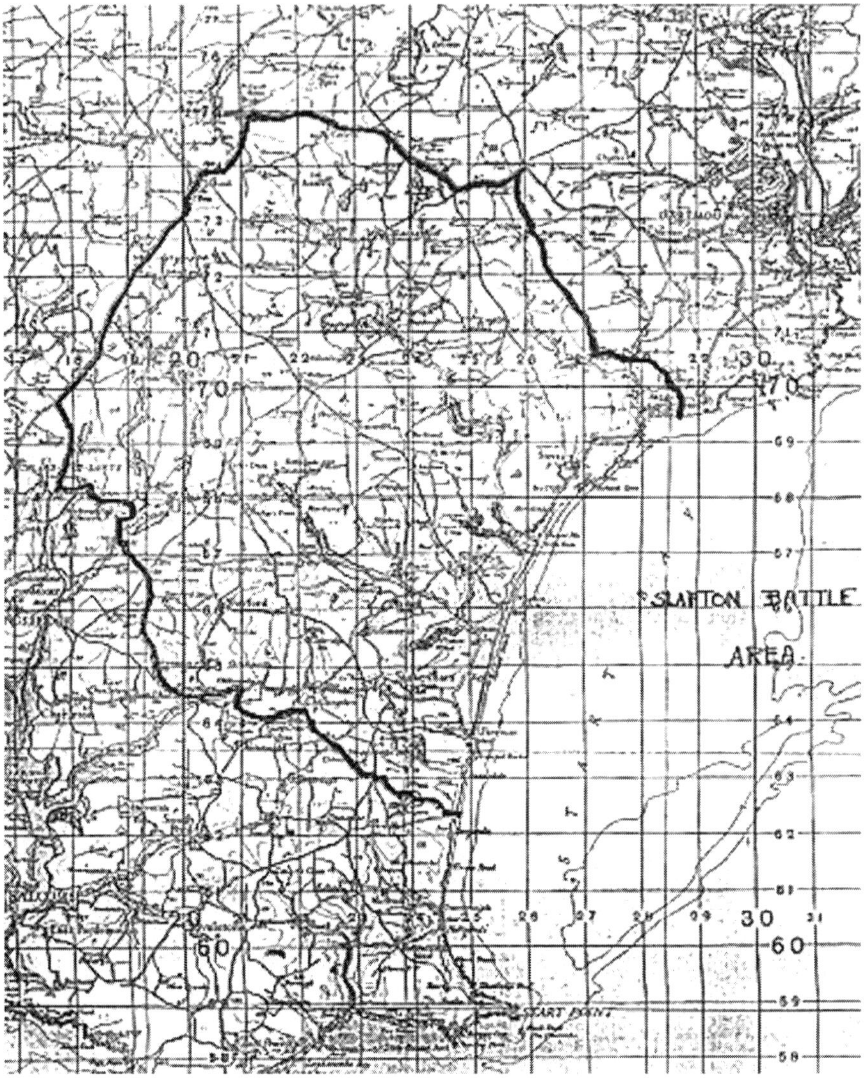

The U.S. command structure of land forces for the Normandy landings placed responsibility for all army units destined for "Omaha" beach with V Corps, and with VII Corps for those assaulting "Utah" beach including paratroops who would land behind "Utah" beach before the seaborne assault to secure vital crossroads, bridges and towns.

Two American amphibious landing rehearsals for the assaults upon "Omaha" and "Utah" beaches were planned to take place at the Slapton battle area in south Devon, England during April and May

1944. These were both codenamed "Fabius" and the first of these was further codenamed "Tiger" under the overall command of U.S. Admiral Don P. MOON.

This was a seven day, dry-run rehearsal for all army and navy units destined to assault "Utah" beach in Normandy to test every aspect of the "Utah" invasion plan. Running from 22nd to 29th April 1944 Exercise "Tiger" was not a training exercise, as every participating army unit was by now fully trained.

Infantry, tanks, engineers and signals were to be convoyed from their home stations to marshalling areas then loaded onto Navy vessels at south Devon ports and harbours for the sea voyage to Slapton Sands.

Movement and loading timetables had to be precise and co-ordinated between the army, air force and navy, a situation that had historically been difficult but was now tested to the extreme.

The rehearsal was to be as realistic as possible with a few exceptions. Airborne troops would not parachute in due to a lack of suitable aircraft and fear of casualties, instead they would be trucked to their mission destinations to hold crossroads and bridges until relieved by seaborne infantry pushing inland.

Some tanks were to be landed from the sea but most would drive to the beach area as infantry support then withdraw once it was judged that a sufficiently strong beachhead had been established.

Twenty four hours after the seaborne assault to establish that beachhead, elements to reinforce, enlarge and consolidate it would land from a second convoy and provide support services necessary for the advance inland.

Casualty numbers

EXERCISE "Tiger" became a disaster involving the deaths of many participating American soldiers and sailors, and the most controversial element of this notorious wartime tragedy is the true number of those casualties.

This has been debated long and hard, all arguments and estimates vehemently defended and promoted by those who have some knowledge, those whose task is to spread mis-information, and by others who have been blindly led by what they have read or been told in popular media forums. The latter may be forgiven as many incorrect facts are repeatedly copied and publicised and with no available counter arguments, until now, they are accepted as truth.

All these debates, conclusions and arguments are hollow and meaningless as they are all based upon available records which leave much to be desired in terms of accuracy, completeness and truth. Contributing to this dearth of hard facts are U.S. military and archive sources whose reluctance or inability to offer a full and comprehensive list of casualties naturally leads to the popular supposition of a "cover–up" to disguise the true losses, believed by many to be far greater than officially admitted.

Theories of casualty numbers from vociferous "experts" all fail basic scrutiny, their proponents falling back upon the excuse of a cover-up or the "fog of war" to explain their inability to fill the gaps and shortcomings of their arguments.

Such wild theories are fuelled by the U.S. military archive's floundering response to any request for clarity of casualty numbers leading to two possibilities. Firstly, they know there really is a deliberate cover-up to conceal the fact there were many more of their soldiers and sailors killed during this D-Day rehearsal than they officially proclaim. Alternatively, they simply just don't know, in which case their ignorance bears the embarrassment of being the victims of a masterful concealment by their predecessors or, more unlikely, the shame of poor record keeping at the time.

In defence of a cover-up, in 2012, R. Scott MOORE, PhD, Chief, Field Programs and Historical Services of the U.S. Army Center of Military History stated ... "*No doubt the events at Slapton Sands occurred and were tragic, and no doubt numbers of soldiers and sailors died that night. But beyond an initial blackout of information to protect the security of pending invasion, no attempt has been made since to cover up those events nor minimize the casualties*".

This carefully structured response using the words "*that night*" – referring to 27th / 28th April 1944 – restricts MOORE's explanation to the German E-Boat attack upon the second convoy, "T-4".

The most vocal "experts" and commenters of Exercise "Tiger" have also concentrated on the German E-Boat ambush of convoy T-4 and assigned 749 casualties to this incident, conveniently omitting the additional 198 U.S. Navy casualties. They have failed to look deeper into the whole exercise for doing so has proved there were two incidents that inflicted casualties during this exercise. The sinking of two LSTs but also something that happened the day before on 27th April 1944.

Based upon detailed analysis of existing records and with exclusive access to unique private documents this is a part-dramatisation of actual events and recollections of those that were part of the event and following actions.

Prepare to move

BEFORE dawn each day from 18th to 22nd April 1944 throughout the south western shires of England hundreds of truck engines coughed into life in the damp spring air creating a lingering blue smoke haze that swirled between the surrounding huts and tents.

Breakfast was finished, equipment and weapons had been collected from sleeping quarters and now it was time to board the waiting trucks. Officers began shouting at sergeants, sergeants were shouting at men who began running to their parade spots, some dropping equipment, some still puling on their combat harness but all of them thinking "*Here we go again*".

Briefed the previous night with the minimum of details, none knew this exercise was an exact dry-run of their real invasion plan. To the ordinary soldier this was just another exercise in a long string of exercises over the past year which, in the average soldier's estimation was all quite pointless and only offered the non-commissioned officers an opportunity to shout even more, and gave the officers an excuse to be finicky about the state of uniforms, weapons and equipment which everyone knew were already perfect.

But there was an unstoppable timetable of events for the next week and this was only the beginning. Over twenty five thousand soldiers were to be moved from camps scattered throughout the two counties of Devon and Cornwall by truck convoys to converge on marshalling areas just outside their D-Day embarkation ports of Plymouth, Dartmouth, Torquay and Brixham.

Over the next few days soldiers, jeeps, trucks, DUKWs, half-tracks, trailers and tanks would be routed in a strict, timed sequence down to the loading hards at harbours and docks to be loaded onto Navy craft.

At Bodmin camp in Cornwall the 33rd Chemical Decontamination Company had been told they would be part of a follow-up convoy, loading at the little fishing port of Brixham onto ships that would take them on a twenty four hour sea voyage into the English Channel. Landing at Slapton Sands on the 28th of April just twenty four hours after the beach assault they were to move inland as directed. And they all knew what that meant. Dig a foxhole, get it just the way you want it then be told "*you're on the move again – so fill it in*".

Almost seven hundred men of the 3rd Battalion, 8th Infantry Regiment left Honiton on trucks at 08:10 on 23rd April 1944 for Torquay, Devon where the next day they would board the attack transport ship HMS "Empire Gauntlet". An hour later the 2nd Battalion of over seven hundred men left the requisitioned Warner holiday camp at Seaton, Devon for the same destination but to board the USS "Barnett" and an hour after that the 1st Battalion left Honiton, Devon, to board the USS "Joseph T. Dickman".

These two thousand infantrymen were to be the first waves to land on Slapton beach opening Exercise "Tiger" at H-Hour on 27th April 1944, an exact replication of their D-Day mission to land on "Utah" beach.

At Camp K-3, Shiphay, Torquay, about two miles from the harbour soldiers were dropped from their trucks into a number of fields covered with large olive drab accommodation tents but it was larger tents with narrow chimneys exuding thin wisps of grey smoke that took their attention. These were the easily recognised cookhouse tents where army cooks were yet again attempting to create edible meals from standard army ration packs plus any other ingredients they had managed to scrounge or barter locally.

Service of Supply Sergeants gathered groups of the disembarked combat troops, led them down avenues between rows of tents shouting names, waving an arm left or right as they did so, glancing occasionally down to clipboards holding lists of personnel, not once pausing or facing the column of men jogging behind them. At the avenue's end, without fail each sergeant turned to face a bewildered group of soldiers who clearly hadn't been paying attention to name calling and arm directions, and now had to interpret the sergeant's shoulder shrug as he marched off tucking the clipboard under his arm.

But everyone had a hot meal and found a cot for the night until 06:00 reveille and parade when further instructions prepared the men for a timetable of marching through the town of Torquay to the loading hards by the harbour.

Loading

AS MARCHING columns of soldiers moved along the traffic-free roads through Torquay town they waved and cat-called to girls on the sidewalk, cheeked the constable on point duty as they passed, talking to each other and grinning as they marched downhill in their own relaxed style.

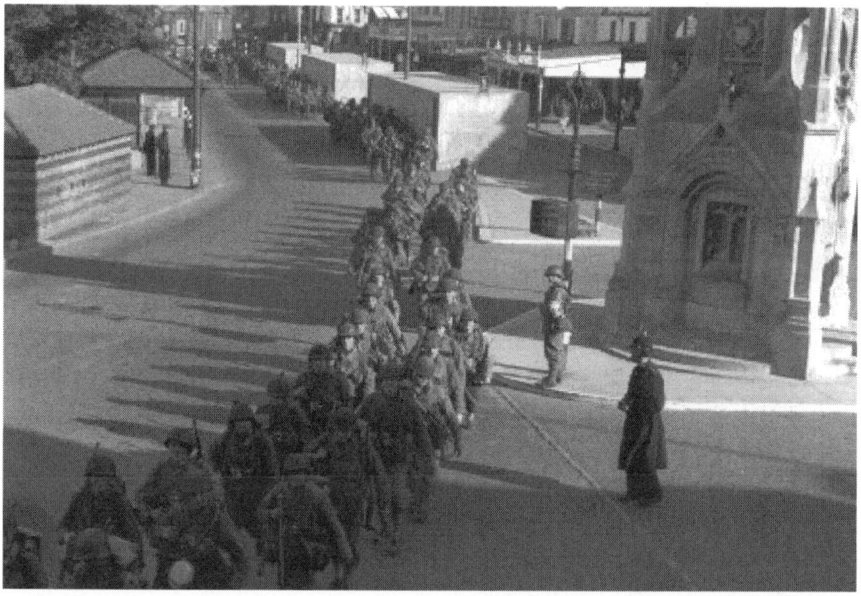

Columns of soldiers coming to a very informal halt at the top of the loading hards were met by U.S. Navy sailors who began counting the soldiers into groups then herding them down the concrete ramp into large landing craft gently moving from side to side pivoting on their ramp lowered onto the concrete as the engine at slow speed ahead kept the ramp hard ashore.

Beyond these stationary LCMs was a column of craft lumbering awkwardly across the swell making their way out to three large, grey attack transport ships anchored about half a mile offshore. To their left was another column of empty landing craft bouncing towards the harbour rising up on each swell before crashing down in white spray. For those prone to sea-sickness this did not look encouraging.

The navy crammed soldiers into the craft well beyond their safe capacity, leaving men so tightly packed standing up that none could fall over as it pitched and rolled on the short voyage out to the transport ships.

Once secured alongside soldiers began the precarious climb up cargo nets to the ship's deck, compelled to time the beginning of their climb against the rise and fall of their craft in relation to the climbing nets, grateful they only carried weapons and combat equipment.

Once aboard they were directed to different accommodation parts of the ship below deck by sailors grinning at the discomfort of those already suffering from sea-sickness.

The loading operation was going smoothly unlike the experience a few miles across Torbay at the small port of Brixham.

Dale Rodman of the 33rd Chemical Decontamination Company as part of a 32 man party had boarded LST 507 via Berth "B" with 175 men of the 557th Quartermaster Railhead Company and 22 DUKWs driven aboard by 45 men of the 478th Amphibious Truck Company during the afternoon of 24th April 1944. They had already found their quarters below deck and while squabbling over bunks were drawn to the top deck by an unholy row on the quayside.

Dale and his companions leaned on the rail and taking great delight as any soldier did in watching confusion, pointed to officers who were clearly in an agitated state as confused columns of infantry moved about the dockside faithfully following each contradictory order.

Eventually these 345 dockside infantrymen of the 8th and 22nd Infantry Regiments walked onto LST 507 and as no preparations had been made for their accommodation, began claiming sheltered corners on the top deck and beneath the parked DUKWs.

They were the scheduled load for LST 508 that had been due to load at the same time on Berth "D" alongside LST 507 and land on "Tare Green" beach, Slapton on the exercise's 3rd tide during 28th April 1944.

But 508 hadn't made it to Brixham. Encountering dense fog with fifty yard visibility while making its way from Fowey, Cornwall, the previous day it had collided with a British merchant ship. It was only a port to port glancing blow but had punched a hole in the hull of LST 508, ripped off the anchor and sprung one of the bow doors making them unusable. LST 508 continued her journey to anchor in Torbay at 10:00 p.m. where closer inspection confirmed she was unable to take part in the exercise and the decision made to return to Falmouth the next day for dry-dock repairs.

The fateful decision was therefore taken that the majority of 508's personnel load should embark on LST 507. It was too late to create a new manifest for LST 507 as the loading hards had a tight loading schedule and 507's space there was urgently needed so she closed the bow doors and withdrew into the harbour.

In Dartmouth soldiers marched from their overnight encampment in their inimitable casual style to the ships at the loading hards, some rolling English pennies down the steep road laughing as the local children raced after the coins.

Numbers already chalked on the front of their helmets were checked against loading lists on the quayside and men shoved up the steep gangways onto the ships that would convoy them out into the English Channel for a short sea voyage before landing them on Slapton beach "under battle conditions".

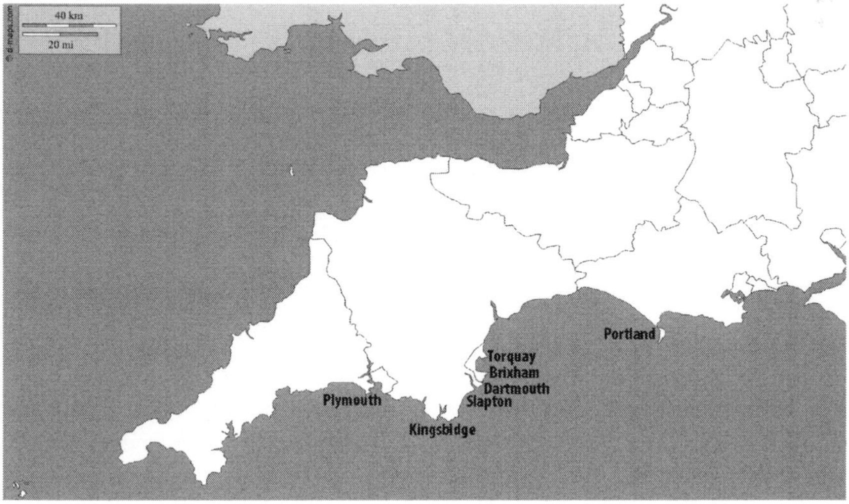

H-Hour delayed

DEEP inside the USS Bayfield, Admiral Moon's exercise flagship, the hushed operations room was bathed in subdued lighting except for the central map table illuminated by low spotlights. Shirt sleeved ratings sat at work stations around the edge, some wearing radio set headphones, others coding and decoding messages to enter details upon the situation chalkboard.

Two petty officers constantly prowled the room perimeter looking over the shoulders of the seated ratings to maintain an up to date overview of the exercise progress and ensure this was available to operational staff officers.

It was now 0430 hours 27th April with H-Hour only two hours ahead when troops of the 8th Infantry Regiment would lead the assault upon Slapton Sands. Already transport ships were signalling they had lowered their landing craft and troops were loading into them.

Disturbing the calm but tense atmosphere the door suddenly opened and Admiral Moon strode to the map table followed by most of his staff officers crowding around him. "*The Army tell me their DD tanks aren't here and won't arrive for another hour*". He was clearly annoyed having already lost one LST of the second convoy at Brixham due to being damaged and unable to participate in the exercise so had ordered those troops to be double loaded onto another LST already in Brixham.

He knew the tanks were a vital element of the initial assault and their absence would affect the efficiency of the whole rehearsal.

Staff officers stepped back from the map table as Moon paced around it with hands on hips, glaring at symbols and marks on the chart indicating every ship was where they were supposed to be and everything was running according to timetable. Now the Army threatened to jeopardise his smooth operation as they insisted the tanks were vital to rehearse infantry / tank co-operation.

There was nothing else he could do. "*Postpone H-Hour by one hour*". Leaning on the table he looked up at his communications officer "*Make sure all ships are informed*".

Pursing his lips with frustration Moon swept out of the operations room leaving his staff to re-schedule the entire exercise. Revised orders were scribbled and put before the communications sailors to transmit coded message "WHISKERS" to all ships, American transport and British warships.

The run-in

THREE APA Attack Transports of convoy T1A left the shelter of Torbay late on 26th April 1944. USS Barnett coded APA 33 had 724 men of the 2nd Battalion, 8th Infantry Regiment on board.

USS Joseph T Dickman coded APA 13 had 763 men of the 1st Battalion and HMS Empire Gauntlet on loan to the U.S. Navy had 879 men of the 3rd Battalion on board.

USS Barnett – APA 5

To escort them to Slapton Sands were three Royal Navy destroyers. HMS Offa built in 1940 which had taken part in the Arctic convoys. HMS Onslaught built in 1942 escorted convoys in the North Atlantic and Arctic, and HMS Oribi which had taken part in a commando raid on Norway. With them were three U.S. Navy patrol craft, PC 484, 1176 and 1261.

Once in the Slapton Sands area these escort vessels all had separate tasks. The destroyers were to bombard Slapton beach then withdraw and form part of the protective screen patrolling a line from Portland Bill extending south westwards tasked with preventing any enemy seaborne incursion into the exercise area.

The patrol craft with others escorting convoys from Plymouth and Brixham were to act as guides for landing craft leaving the APAs as they headed for Slapton Sands beaches "Uncle Red" and "Tare Green". PC 1261 commanded by Lt Floyd Sewell, USNR was the

"Primary Control Craft", PC 80 the "Secondary Control Craft" and PC 90 the Tertiary for "Uncle Red".

Troops aboard the APAs anchored at "Point X-Ray" in the transport area pinpointed 10.3 miles from Start Point Light bearing 273 degrees true, were roused and fed breakfast and after a final equipment check, climbed over the ships rails and down cargo nets into LCVPs tenaciously holding station alongside as they rose and fell with the sea swell.

Standard procedure was for loaded LCVPs to leave their mother ship, proceed to the "Rendezvous Area" arriving thirty minutes before their due time of departure. There they would proceed in circles abreast of the static secondary and tertiary control vessels. Odd numbered waves rotating in numerical sequence in a clockwise direction and even numbered waves in an anti-clockwise direction.

Once LCVP waves were complete and ready the tertiary control vessel would hoist a wave number. Hauling it down was the signal that wave number was to proceed towards the beachline and the "Line of Departure" 3,500 yards off the beach guided by "Reference vessels" Able (ML 118), Baker (ML 153), Charlie (ML 163) and Dog (ML 304). Their departure from the rendezvous area was radioed in clear to the command ship USS Bayfield as "departure".

First waves of LCVPs were led by the "Secondary Control Craft" until it was 2,000 yards off the beach at which point it reversed course which was the signal for the LCVPs to head for the beach by themselves.

On "Uncle Red Beach" the 8th Infantry Regiment LCVPs were deployed as follows:-

	Wave 1	*Wave 2*	*Wave 4*	*Wave 5*	*Wave 6*
Leave Rendezvous	H-105	H-98	H-80	H-65	H-55
Leave Line of departure	H-12	H-5	H+13	H+28	H+38
Land	H-Hour	H+7	H+25	H+40	H+50

Companies "E" and "F" were in Wave 1, Company G of 2nd Battalion, 8th Infantry Regiment were in Wave 2.

Unknown to any of the circling LCVPs or control craft was that H-Hour had been delayed by one hour. Despite Admiral Moon's order that message hadn't filtered down the communication channels to them.

Hitting the beach

CROUCHED in each hold of ten LCVPs were thirty infantrymen of Companies "E" and "F" 8th Infantry Regiment. They had been there for over an hour and a half riding out the bucking craft's every gut-wrenching lurch, pitch and roll, now being sprayed with salt water each time their craft fell into the sea swell's trough.

Originally allowed to stand and steady themselves against the vessel sides they had watched the other LCVPs maneuver into a line abreast behind Patrol Craft #80 as they approached their line of departure almost two miles from Slapton beach.

Suddenly PC80 in front of them came about and made full speed back to the transport area, signalling the LCVPs were on their own for the beach. Men were ordered into their crouching position and craft lurched as helmsmen gunned their engines and finally made full speed for the beach.

Each LCVP helmsman occasionally glanced left and right to maintain position in the line while concentrating on the approaching coastline, picking out features of the silhouette they'd been shown at their briefing to ensure a landing at the correct spot on "Uncle Red" beach.

Almost together the ten LCVPs of the first wave navy-coded "22UR" to "31UR" hit the beach in the right place and on time – 06:30.

Each shuddered to a stop as they hit the shingle beach followed instantly by a rumble, and a scream of metal against metal from cables as the ramps were released, dropping with a huge splash and suddenly exposing the view of a steep shingle bank to the soldiers who surged forward into shallow water and to their relief, onto dry land.

It wasn't easy running up the steep beach in ankle-deep, loose gravel, but exactly as they'd been taught at the Assault Training Center they fanned out and reached the top of the beach incline to lie flat and assess their positions as the first wave to step ashore. Seven minutes behind them at sea the second wave could be seen ploughing through the waves towards them.

Hardly anyone had noticed the lack of a beach bombardment in the confusion and noise of their trip from ship to shore, those that did shrugged it off as yet another exercise foul-up.

Simultaneous shouted orders caused all three hundred men to rise together and move across the ridge onto level ground. Many were stopped in their tracks, crumpled and fell back down the beach as they were hit by a curtain of bullets from rifles and machine guns of the U.S. 1st Infantry Division dug in on the hill beyond the freshwater lake in front of them.

Survivors pressed forward with their attack as training took over but the advance stalled as they sought cover and shelter as more men fell. A few wondered if rumours were true and this really was the invasion and not just an exercise.

In the second wave 150 men of Company "G" in five LCVPs "37 UR" to "41 UR" hit the beach and made the same laborious run up the beach, around the bodies and onto the ridge, pausing to assess their situation and about to advance behind "E" and "F" Companies when the ground around them began to explode sending splintered gravel at bullet speed in all directions.

It was now 06:40 and right on schedule HMS "Offa" and "Oribi" of "Fire Support Unit 4" opened fire, each firing 30 rounds from their

4.7 inch guns on their designated targets on "Uncle Red" beach – and right on top of the infantry.

Some men were cut open by stone shards, others disappeared in explosions, evaporated or blown apart, some stayed put, frantically digging shallow scrapes in the shingle for cover, others ran over the ridge line only to be cut down by small arms fire from the hill beyond the freshwater lake.

They had nowhere to go and there was no going back, the craft had all pulled away heading back to the rendezvous area and their next load of infantry.

Men hugged the gravel beach face down, some occasionally screamed and rolled over clutching bloody wounds, others were flung into the air falling with contorted limbs to lay still and lifeless or scream in agony.

Captain James Haley commanding G Company had a direct radio link to HMS "Oribi" and shouted into his radioman's handset for the naval guns to cease fire yet it still took a few deadly minutes for the naval gunfire to stop.

From Company G's bitter experience it is obvious that the message delaying H-Hour by one hour had not reached any of the Control vessels, Reference vessels or USS Barnett which continued to load LCVPs.

During the exercise debrief Admiral Moon agreed with General Collins that ... "*communication is all important. Do not plan on radio communication during the assault*". His inexperience as an amphibious

commander was highlighted by his admission that ... " *Regarding H-Hour. Took on DD boats. Said it will be an hour before they could be in. I made a poor decision. Learned a great deal by this delay in H Hour*".

But the H-Hour delay message had reached some vessels. Two rocket firing LCTs (366 and 368) in their after-action report stated they "*were not allowed to fire due to the fact that isolated units of the first wave, which did not get the message that H-Hour was postponed, landed one hour before H-Hour*".

Testimony from a Company G, 2nd Battalion, 8th Infantry Regiment, 4th Infantry Division veteran … "*G Company assaulted the beach as they had practiced previously, and as soon as they landed they started receiving fire from our Navy. The Navy had not received word that G had landed, and they were shelling the beach. G Company commander, Captain James HALEY, radioed the Navy to stop shelling, which they did*".

Ray MANN of G Company also remembers that landing … "*When we did land we were almost wiped out by our own Navy. Things were screwed up and we landed before the Naval bombardment. We just got on the beach when the Navy started to fire. Captain HALEY saved our day*".

Major Edwin WOLF of the 6th Engineer Special Brigade was an onshore observer to Exercise "Tiger" who vividly remembers seeing the first waves of infantry landing, falling down, and not moving. Realising they were being shot and killed by the "defenders" WOLF raced along the lines shouting for the firing to cease but by that time many casualties already lay on the beach and in the surf of Slapton Sands.

"*There was overhead fire from the troops posing as enemy troops on shore which was not anticipated by the landing troops coming ashore and I regret to say there were a number of casualties. When I saw what was going on I knew something was wrong, I tried to do something about it but I had no command position*".

Glyn Hiscock was a Royal Marine aboard HMS Hawkins "*We approached the bombardment area and carried out our bombardment shoot at the beach. H-Hour had been retarded by an hour but some troops and equipment had got ashore. We heard later that morning that there had been 200 casualties*".

James CORY was driver to a British army officer attached to the American forces at Slapton Sands "*On the morning of 27th April 1944 there were between four and five hundred of these Americans were acting as "Germans", they were defending and they were placed along the sand dunes and cliffs. And as they (attacking troops) started running up the beach these defenders started opening fire and they started going down like ninepins. When my officer shouted at their officer in charge he said "well that's my orders – keep firing". As we left I counted 150 bodies on the beach".*

Despite this carnage on the beach the exercise timetable was unstoppable and wave after wave of landing craft and ships continued disgorging troops and vehicles for the next few hours. No comments have been heard from soldiers passing those bodies on the beach but they knew there was a casualty evacuation practice element within the exercise and probably assumed these were part of it.

It was only later in the day when most elements had moved far inland that bodies on the beach attracted attention.

Dale SEES, an engineer sergeant "*saw approximately 2 hundred or more fatal casualties, some scattered on the beach and some piled in groups. I saw 6x6 trucks, tarp covered, and with tarp curtains in rear, being loaded with fatal casualties. I mentioned this to my officer and he said they were moving them to an inland cemetery".*

Despite clearing bodies on the beach, some were drifting in and out with the tide and to clear them Royal Navy LCA 803 Flotilla based at Dartmouth, Devon, were mobilised and tasked with urgently collecting them for several days afterwards before the next "Fabius" exercise due to commence on 2nd May 1944.

Private Ivor BEALEY of the British engineers liaison group stated the beach was ... "*knee deep*" with bodies and he had ... "*been loading bodies from the beach onto a lorry for a pastime*".

American serviceman Harold McAulley revealed how he buried bodies – their faces black with oil and burns – in the South Hams. He said: "*We hauled them off the beach and took a couple of (truck) loads inland and just threw them in.*"

One local man to Slapton Sands remembers he ... "*helped to assemble and load up bodies of soldiers into army trucks which then took the dead off into the countryside above Slapton*".

Mass burials

FEW local people involved ever spoke about that day but local rumour in south Devon persisted that American soldiers were buried in a field "*behind Slapton Ley*", and in the 1980s these stories surfaced in a west country newspaper interviewing local woman Dorothy SEEKINGS who insisted she had witnessed bodies in trucks being put into a large pit dug in a field.

She was publicly ridiculed by local people and attempts made to have her story discredited by attention seeking individuals pretending to have personal knowledge of the secret of bodies buried in the South

Tiger tragedy: Are the victims buried in a South Hams field?

by SUE MORGAN

The mystery which shrouds the final resting place of young Americans who perished off the Devon coast during the war, has thrown the spotlight onto an ordinary housewife, the mighty Pentagon, an hotelier with a mission and even a millionaire author.

But the only person who could hold the key to the 40-year-old riddle of the sands, won't talk about it. Nolan Tope, the Blackawton farmer whose field was remembered as the windswept spot where dead US Servicemen were lowered into mass graves after a full scale invasion rehearsal turned into a real enemy attack, is reluctant to dig up the past.

Speculation on whether the remains of some of the 750 dead from the Exercise Tiger tragedy of April 28, 1944 might still lie under South Hams farmland, has reached no watertight conclusion.

After more than three years of questions since civilian Dorothy Seekings of Stoke Fleming broke her wartime vow of silence to US military men and told how she witnessed bodies for burial in Nolan Tope's field a few weeks before D-Day, the answers leave a nagging element of doubt.

The US military has maintained since the questions began, that no American Servicemen lie forgotten in fields near the wartime training area of Slapton Sands.

And the Tope family is not inclined to settle any doubts. Nolan Tope's wife is adamant that the field should not be disturbed. "If they are there, then let them rest in peace," she said.

BODIES MYSTERY: Dorothy Seekings points to the field in which she claims Tiger tragedy victims were buried.

US memorial

At the US Military Cemetery in Cambridge there are 293 Tiger victims on the solemn "Wall of the Missing" — war dead whose remains were never found or were unidentified. One

ments Commission representative in Britain, stated that after World War II, US Army teams were sent to temporary graves to collect the remains for reburial.

But Mrs. Seekings disputes that US troops returned to the evacuated area after D-Day.

Mr. Prieur feels it "very unlikely" that any remains might still lie in hastily-dug wartime graves in Devon. Of the 293 listed as missing, he said: "Maybe the currents took their bodies [illegible] to the high seas." Certainly local people do not remember any bodies washed up on South Devon beaches.

Mr Prieur recently visited the site at

bombed-out radio transmission tower near Plymouth."

More than 300 casualties from Tiger were transported by truck to the small Brookwood American Cemetery at Woking near London, the former member of the US Army graves registration company disclosed.

These were exhumed between 1946 and 1948 and taken to the World War II American military cemetery at Cambridge, a spokesman at Brookwood said.

The "bodies question" is still discussed, sometimes with furtive looks, by elderly South Hams people who returned to their evacuated homes

wind-blown cut corn, my elderly guide told me quietly: "You are now standing on top of it."

But subsequent investigations revealed that the "body-filled bunker" is a Royal Observer Corps underground monitoring centre built after the war and still used.

The strict military secrecy which surrounded the pre-D-Day tragedy at the time, seems to have had a lasting copy-cat effect on many older South Hams people. "We were always told — what you hear, keep under your hat," an evacuated resident said.

Sherman tank

Hams fields and to have secret information they were not prepared to disclose.

Some dramatised their supposed knowledge for the benefit of the aroused media interest only to stop short of any detail when pressed for more information proving they knew nothing and were merely seeking attention.

Dorothy Seeking's father was a local baker and one of the few people permitted to travel the edge of the Slapton Battle Area as he supplied bread and doughnuts to the American Service of Supply guards patrolling the perimeter. Dorothy was often seen helping her father with deliveries and at the end of April 1944, walking along the quiet road towards Blackawton she was recognised and offered a ride in the cab of a large American army truck.

When it stopped by a gateway just short of Wadstray House she climbed down and walking to the truck rear saw bodies piled on the floor. Looking in the gateway she saw more trucks in the field unloading bodies into huge pits being dug by a solitary bulldozer.

Years later the site she had indicated to the newspaper was pinpointed behind Wadstray House, Blackawton, and initial exploratory excavation revealed grave cuts and one buried U.S. army uniform button indicating these rumours are indeed fact and Dorothy SEEKINGS was telling the truth.

Further exploration of that field was planned with the land owner's permission as part of a TV documentary telling the truth of Exercise Tiger. During filming for the programme in the United States the

production team had a "chance" encounter with Congressman Scott Rigell of Virginia who showed great interest in the story.

Returning to England to film the field exploration the TV production team were informed by the land owner, who had always been most supportive, that he "*had changed his mind*" and withdrawn his permission.

This congressional intervention may have achieved an official objective of preventing further excavation of the burial site but confirms there really is something to hide in those Devon fields.

Casualties of the German E-Boat attack were killed or drowned miles from Slapton Sands their bodies at the mercy of tides and currents all flowing eastwards so it is unlikely the bodies buried at Blackawton come from this disaster, they have to be from those first units ashore on 27th April – the 8th Infantry Regiment.

While physical proof cannot now be obtained by excavation there are many witnesses in addition to Dorothy SEEKINGS, all offering proof positive that bodies were buried at Blackawton.

Tantalising aerial photographs of the Blackawton area taken in 1945/46 show ground disturbance at Wadstray and other areas, suggesting mass burials were made at more than one site.

Tip off

THE beaches of Normandy had been selected as the landing grounds for the Allied invasion of Europe and tight security had kept that secret from the Germans who could only guess where the Allies would land.

Their logical conclusion was somewhere in the vicinity of Calais. It was the shortest distance from the English coast and offered vast, open sandy beaches ideal for an amphibious landing.

With no apparent practical or strategic alternatives the German decision was to keep the majority of their best troops and armour in the vicinity of Calais, something the Allies wished to maintain.

Operation Fortitude was an intricate and complex web of Allied deceit and physical deceptions to mislead and confuse the Germans of Allied intentions. To achieve this, the master plan was divided into North and South with two vastly differing scenarios. The North plan was to convince the Germans of an invasion of Norway and the South to prepare the way for the invasion of Normandy.

Within Fortitude South was Operation Bodyguard specifically tasked with convincing the Germans that the Allied invasion of Europe would be in the Pas de Calais area and to divert German attention away from Normandy.

At the core of this crucial effort were a handful of European misfits who for their own personal and peculiar reasons inveigled themselves into German confidence, offered to work for them as spies in England and remarkably were accepted.

They were self-centred, inefficient, had no dedication to the Nazi cause apart from two exceptions and completely lacking in patriotism or allegiance to any country and poorly equipped for their task.

From 1939 to 1942 many surrendered themselves almost as soon as they landed in England the remainder were so inept and poorly prepared for wartime Britain they were tracked down within days of arriving.

But instead of execution or incarceration they were recognised as a potentially valuable asset. Interrogated by the British secret service their suitability to be "turned" and work for the British was assessed during which the hint must have been given that they could be tried for treason with an inevitable verdict of guilty and death by shooting or hanging. Alternatively they were offered the opportunity of sending false information to Berlin under the supervision of the British secret services.

Almost all of them opted to live and transmit false intelligence for their new masters under the control of Thomas "Tar" Argyll Robertson of MI5. He quickly recognised to establish their credibility was vital to deter Germany from sending any more spies and he personally urged Prime Minister Winston Churchill to use them in a double-cross programme. His approval was subject to agreement by General Dwight D. Eisenhower who was responsible for the execution of deception plans in his theatre of operations in Fortitude South.

It was a delicate and difficult task to include snippets of genuine information intertwined with deception material without the genuine details being of use to the Germans and it was always a concern that some messages may be too subtle and escape the German attention they sought but thanks to the Enigma code being broken at Bletchley Park, German responses could be monitored.

Before Operation "Torch", the invasion of North Africa, genuine information was included in a letter to Berlin from turned agent "Garbo", falsely postmarked before the invasion and deliberately delayed so as to arrive after the troops had landed. Berlin was naturally disappointed with the letter's late arrival but the contents persuaded Berlin to give firm credibility to "Garbo".

As D-Day approached and the turned spies into full swing with Operation Fortitude the higher military commands became increasingly reluctant to allow the slightest hint of true information being fed to Berlin no matter how it was presented.

All the turned spies could do now was transmit pitiful details of their "sightings" of army insignia, vehicle markings and bar room chatter to the point that Robertson was becoming concerned his efforts to convince Berlin that Calais was the Allied objective may not be working. Despite positive Enigma decodes he worried that Berlin may lose faith in "their" spy network which, under his supervision were doing their utmost to persuade Berlin that Calais really was the Allies' objective.

What he needed to consolidate his spy's credibility beyond doubt to convince and assure Berlin their future transmissions about Calais would be true and accurate was a piece of genuine information.

Then a chilling decision was made at the very highest level to send that one piece of genuine information. Its timing was important. It had to be made sufficiently in advance of the projected invasion date of late May or early June 1944 to allow movement of enemy forces to withdraw from Normandy and make their way to the Calais area.

The problem of what situation the Allies could present to the Germans to successfully achieve this was solved by simply hinting at the time and place of a genuine military exercise in the English Channel which had the added bonus of perhaps confusing the Germans into believing the real invasion was under way.

Many small scale amphibious training exercises had already been carried out by American forces in their battle exercise area at Slapton in south Devon from December 1943 and the only remaining planned exercises within the critical time frame were to be full-scale rehearsals by navy and army task forces destined for invading Normandy.

This was the "Fabius" exercise series, the first sub-coded "Tiger" scheduled for late April for naval and army forces destined to land on "Utah" beach. Exercises for other forces were scheduled afterwards but were judged too late to achieve a withdrawal of enemy units from Normandy, especially armoured divisions which were considered the greatest threat to establishing an Allied beachhead.

Exercise "Tiger" was therefore selected as the subject of this disinformation ploy. Allied intelligence suggested that E-Boats would be the greatest threat to any Channel shipping so to minimise the risk measures were put in place including several defensive lines of Royal Navy ships as a screen way out in the Channel. Additionally Royal Navy motor torpedo boats would patrol between them and the American convoy as well as small craft patrols outside the E-Boat base at Cherbourg.

In hindsight Royal Navy Director of Tactical, Torpedo and Staff Duties Division commented upon the reliance placed upon these defensive measures "*The system of patrol lines which looks so solid and comforting on a chart is in fact an ensnaring myth of security yet one in which a sublime faith is invariably put*". Those privy to the betrayal of convoy T4 had indeed been persuaded they provided sufficient protection.

The Royal Navy would be protecting two American convoys for Exercise "Tiger", the first carrying assault troops, the second carrying reinforcements. To minimise the risk of losing precious combat troops the second convoy coded "T-4" was further chosen as the subject of this unique deception.

Lieutenant General Frederick Morgan as Chief of Staff to the Supreme Allied Commander (COSSAC) oversaw every detail of the invasion of north western Europe codenamed Operation "Overlord" including diversionary operations to mislead the Germans into believing the Calais area was the true invasion threat so it was his job to inform the Americans.

U.S. Navy Admiral John L. HALL was commander of 11th Amphibious Force responsible for delivering the U.S. Army to their Normandy beaches with the added task of conducting joint training operations with both navy and army. Being the first to be informed of the decision to offer convoy T-4 of Exercise Tiger as bait to the Germans he had to tell his commander of the "Utah" force Admiral Don P. Moon.

Moon had only been appointed in January 1944 as naval commander of the "Utah" force having no experience as an amphibious commander and consequently under great pressure to rapidly and fully understand his role and responsibilities. Relying heavily upon his more experienced staff he was taken aback when Hall informed him on 6th April 1944 what was to happen.

Moon entered Hall's office, saluted and removed his cap. Hall returned the salute, rose from his chair behind the large desk and leaned forward extending his hand to Moon. "*Hello Don, how's it going* ?" gripping and shaking Moon's hand. "*Well thank you sir*" sitting in the chair indicated by Hall who moved round his desk to perch on the front edge, folding his hands in his lap as he faced Moon.

"*I've got to talk to you about your rehearsal – Tiger*" he opened. Moon was instantly cautious suspecting criticism of his planning so responded "*It's all going well, everything is in hand*". Hall took a deep breath while looking directly into Moon's eyes "*The British have introduced another element into it*" leaning forward Moon opened his mouth to enquire but Hall didn't wait for a response. "*They've told the Germans all about it*".

Moon was stunned and fell back in his chair. Struggling to respond he looked rapidly around Halls' office searching for an appropriate response but all he could manage was "*What !*".

"*I don't have details*" said Hall "*but I'm assured they know what they're doing and there are some very real reasons for doing it*". Moon's mouth was open as he stared quizically into Hall's face looking for an explanation, more information – anything. But Hall was keen to end this awkward conversation, rising and returning to his chair he said "*Go see Admiral KIrk – he's got the details but this is top secret, not a word. Incidentally you're doing a grand job*". Hall extended his hand across the desk to Moon who in a state of disbelief ignored it, put on his cap, turned and left the office.

It is uncertain if Hall did know more but embarrassed by the situation brushed off the responsibility of convincing Moon that his first exercise and large scale rehearsal was to be deliberately sabotaged.

The next day Moon and his operations staff officer Captain Moran flew from Plymouth to London to meet with Rear Admiral Alan G. Kirk commander of the Western Naval Task Force and his superior, British Admiral Bertram Ramsay, Naval Commander Allied Expeditionary Force.

Moon and Moran returned to Plymouth on 9th April and Moon was so disturbed by this turn of events to the point he needed his objections to be smoothed over as he took his arguments back to Hall the following day aboard the USS Ancon where they were joined by Sir David Petrie. Petrie as Director General of MI5 was effectively responsible for British national security and was fully aware of the Double Cross operation and best qualified to convince Moon this tip-off was vital to the success of D-Day in Normandy.

It was a decision taken and approved at the very highest level and not something Moon could argue. He was left with no choice and while there is no record of this meeting his protestations must have been considerable in the face of reasoned strategic arguments. All he could do now was attempt to minimise the danger without revealing precisely what that danger was. To achieve this he instructed his staff who were frantically preparing Operational Order 2-44 for Exercise "Tiger" to include in it as frequently as possible the warning that an E-Boat attack was most likely. During briefings MOON attended, he stressed and repeated the same threat was a strong possibility but he dared do no more. All he could now hope for was that the inevitable enemy seaborne attack could be beaten off by ships and craft of the Royal Navy before they came within striking distance of his convoys.

By 24th April 1944 even Admiral Hall was becoming jittery and during a briefing for vessel commanders of Exercise "Tiger" warned them that enemy attack by aircraft, surface craft and submarines may be expected during the exercise.

The Royal Navy was under growing pressure as D-Day approached to keep the English Channel clear of enemy activity by increasing destroyer patrols and mine laying sorties off the Normandy coastline. Their responsibilities extended to protecting all vessels and convoys plying the English Channel so the American demand for protection during their invasion rehearsals added extra strain to their tired and overworked vessels and crews. With so many commitments already this request may have prompted a less than complete response to provide as many ships requested by the American's estimation for adequate screening of their vulnerable unarmed convoys.

Relations between the U.S. and Royal navies were not good with constant arguments and disagreements upon boundaries and levels of responsibilities resulting in furious exchanges of exasperated memorandums attempting to draw definitive accountability. These documents were not always successful in their aim as one ambiguous memorandum was quoted by the Royal Navy in the aftermath of Exercise "Tiger" in the hope of brushing off all responsibility and was rapidly responded to by the U.S. Navy's alternative interpretation of that same document.

Only the highest Allied commanders knew how the Germans successfully located convoy T-4 but what did astonish them was just how successful their attack had been as they considered sufficient preventative measures had been taken to foil a full scale attack by E-Boats.

E-Boat attack

ROBERTSON'S double agents had sent their Exercise Tiger messages to Berlin and he now needed the Germans to interpret them the way he wanted and respond with positive action to verify "their" spy's credibility.

Robertson knew this would happen once the Germans located the American convoy and reassure Berlin that "their" spy's future information was dependable – including his goal of diverting German attention to the Pas de Calais as the Allied intended invasion point.

The German's problem was that with Allied air superiority and sophisticated radar early warning system an air attack was unlikely to succeed. Submarines were still committed far out in the Atlantic but their E-Boat squadrons of 5th and 9th Flotilla at Cherbourg were fully operational and ideally placed for the venture across the English Channel. The same logical conclusions Allied intelligence had already drawn, calculating an E-Boat attack was the most likely response for which adequate defences were in place.

At precisely 10 p.m. on 27th April 1944, nine E-Boats under radio silence and already at action stations slowly made their way westwards from Cherbourg, dropping into formation of two parallel lines before opening throttles to near maximum speed of 36 knots.

Their attack had already been planned from information contained within secret message 2268 and they intended to intercept the Allied convoy 10 miles west of Portland Bill at half past midnight on 28th April 1944.

Passing to the north of the Channel Islands radio silence was broken ordering the columns to turn onto a northerly heading at 11:16 p.m. and just one minute later split into attack formations of two craft per squadron in line abreast.

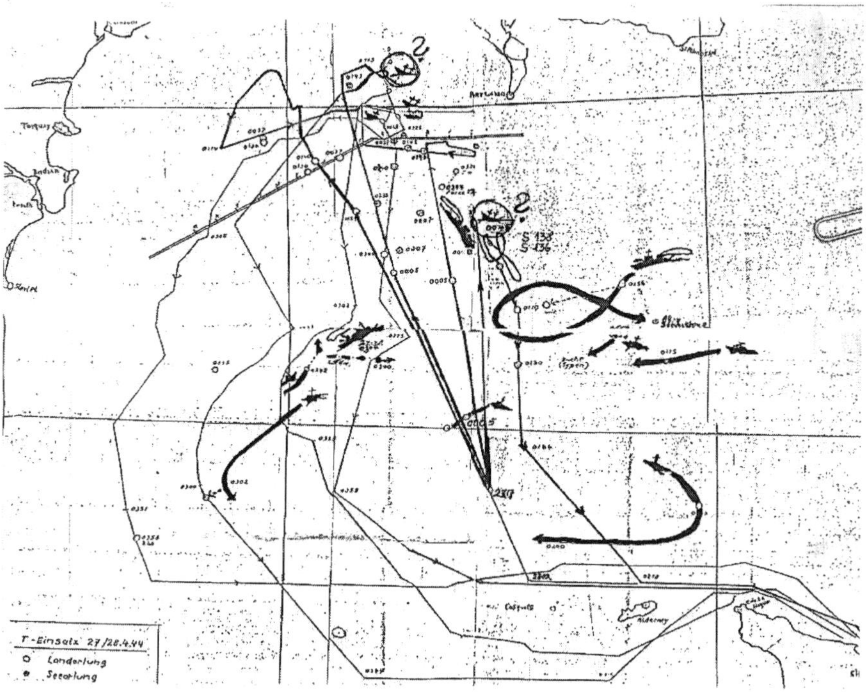

Thirty minutes later E-Boat base control confirmed that by radio direction location their target was exactly where they had predicted it to be and the attack formations continued their advance at high speed skimming over the slight swell, separating ready for attack.

Nearing the anticipated attack area half an hour later S138 of 3 Squadron commanded by Captain Stohwasser spotted the Royal Navy protective screen of "*double smokestack destroyers*" ahead and attacked with torpedoes causing a flash noticed at 3 minutes past midnight by craft of 9 Flotilla behind 3 Squadron and to their left, who assumed it was torpedo hits on a destroyer.

The Allied protective screen ships were too good an opportunity to miss so Stohwasser continued stalking two other destroyers, HMS "Onslow" and "Obedient", and moments later fired two torpedoes at the rearmost ship. He was joined by S136 commanded by Lieutenant Jurgenmeyer who also launched a double shot and in less than a minute heard a terrific explosion, saw flames coming from the destroyer and felt huge shock waves from the explosion. Unknown to them this was a premature detonation of the launched torpedoes as neither ship was damaged but both reported "*fragments fell on board*".

The two E-Boats reversed course to avoid any counter attack then stopped to avoid creating a tell-tale phosphorescent wake and watched the foremost destroyer fire in completely the opposite direction before attempting to go alongside the attacked destroyer then pull away and zig zag to the south east away from the E-Boats.

This was HMS "Onslow" reacting to radio reports from Royal Navy, Portsmouth of shore radar contacts of E-Boats in their vicinity and "Onslow" briefly sighted the E-Boats before passing that information to Admiral Moon aboard his flagship USS "Bayfield".

At 14 minutes past midnight all E-Boat squadrons resumed their original high speed course deep into Lyme Bay leaving S138 to watch the attacked destroyer sink and pick up any survivors. At 12:50 a.m. S138 reported that the destroyer had sunk.

Records show that no Allied destroyers were sunk on 27th or 28th April 1944 in the English Channel but on 29th April HMCS Athabaskan was sunk by German craft off the Britanny coast. Coincidentally the Athabaskan was one of the patrolling destroyers of the security screen for Exercise "Tiger".

Attacking the destroyers had provoked a frantic response from other vessels of the protective screen which steamed aimlessly around the attack area looking for the attackers who were now well inside the protective screen and closing on their original convoy target.

At 1:00 a.m. the LSTs were spotted and the attack was opened by 2 Squadron, S140 launching two torpedoes from 1,800 metres running at a depth of 3 metres, both of which missed, passing ahead of their target. S142 launched two torpedoes at the same ship from 1,400 metres but again missed, trying three more times, all missing their target.

Minutes later 3 Squadron radioed that they were out of ammunition but did loiter in the attack area watching S140 and S142 of 2nd Squadron rake two LSTs with 4cm gunfire which to their surprise provoked no return fire.

Despite the E-Boats torpedo and gunfire attack convoy T-4 continued following their prescribed course at the same slow speed, obediently turning slowly to the south as 3 Squadron's craft made a four-minute parallel high speed run northwards covering them with 4cm gunfire.

The solitary convoy escort HMS "Azalea" was well ahead of the convoy and had been identified by 9 Flotilla craft but it was too far to their stern to make a torpedo attack so S150 and S130 made a joint torpedo attack on an LST while S145 attacked smaller vessels.

At precisely 2:00 a.m. one torpedo hit an LST "*Steamer immediately in bright flames*" and E-Boats opened fire on the blazing ship and to their surprise again received no return fire. Within minutes another LST was hit to the north "*brightly burning with large black smoke billows*".

1 Squadron lined themselves up for a torpedo launch on another LST but was beaten to it by another squadron so targeted the next LST with two torpedoes both of which missed.

S143 sent another two torpedoes at a smaller vessel, both of them hit and the ship was seen to burn and sink.

Targets were everywhere and E-Boats were in danger of colliding as all were manoeuvring at high speed before slowing to launch torpedoes but despite continual evasive action S145 collided with a convoy vessel.

At 2:17 a.m. S150 launched a pair of torpedoes at an LST and "*gets two hits on a steamer which goes up immediately in bright flames*".

By 2:20 a.m. 28th April 1944 the attack was over. E-Boats were almost out of ammunition and had suffered no damage from Allied unco-ordinated fire.

In less than an hour it appeared to the Germans they had sunk one destroyer and three large ships.

Twenty minutes later all E-Boats were on their run home, encountering destroyers in mid Channel maintaining their patrol line, one engaging an E-Boat with heavy fire but disappeared to the north, others were seen heading in the same direction.

Confusion among the Allied destroyers was obvious. On their home run 1 Squadron saw two destroyers ahead of them firing their guns to the south and decided to take advantage of their position and attack them as each boat had two torpedoes left. Slowing to an attack position other destroyers were seen to left and right but the target suddenly turned towards them forcing evasive action but S143 wasn't quick enough and was hit in the stern.

The attack opportunity was gone so 9 Flotilla boats headed for Cherbourg. On their route they were bemused by an Allied destroyer "*firing heavily on a landing ship*", concluding the destroyer wasn't aware of a second convoy in the vicinity.

This incident came about as four American PC Boats escorting a convoy of LSTs, code name "Obstacle" appeared on the radar of HMS "Onslow" and "Obedient". It took precious minutes to identify "Obstacle" as friendly by which time the E-Boats had disappeared.

Approaching Cherbourg from the west the returning E-Boats were warned by their base that due to enemy destroyer activity the coastal batteries were on high alert but by 5:35 a.m. all E-Boats were safely back in Cherbourg harbour.

During the action debrief overseen by Captain von Mirbach the 9th Flotilla leader, it was concluded that two LSTs and one LCT had been sunk. S150 and S130 should be credited each with a half-kill of one LST, one kill of another LST to S150 and the LCT credited to S145.

S100	Captain, BERKENHAGEN	1st Squadron	5th Flotilla
S143	Captain, SCHMALZER	1st Squadron	5th Flotilla
S140	Captain, GOETSCHKE	2nd Squadron	5th Flotilla
S142	Captain, AHRENS	2nd Squadron	5th Flotilla
S136	Captain, Lt JURGENMEYER	3rd Squadron	5th Flotilla
S138	Captain, STOHWASSER	3rd Squadron	5th Flotilla
S150	Captain, BEKE	9th Flotilla	½ kill
(with S130) = 1 kill (damaged)			
S130	Captain, RABE	9th Flotilla	½ kill
(with S150)			
S145	Captain, SCHIRREN	9th Flotilla	1 kill

First reports

A DIM, bare electric light bulb swung gently as the door was opened to the small wooden guard hut, stirring the smoky haze as the U.S. navy sailor stepped inside. "*Cold morning out there*" he muttered, "*Uh-huh*" was the disinterested response from his buddy slumped half asleep on the tipped back, hard wooden chair. "*Your turn, it's three o'clock*" was again met by "*Uh-huh*" as the weary sailor reached for his rifle and swung his feet off the small wooden table. Standing up he cleared his throat and said "*O.K.*" reaching for the door handle he braced himself for the chill as he stepped outside.

He'd been in Plymouth, England, since January 1944 and for the past three months had done nothing but file papers and documents at the U.S. Navy headquarters in Hamoaze House. O.K. some were interesting to read especially the officer's personnel files but it was hard to write home and make it sound as if he was doing something worthwhile to win the war. Now he was on gate guard for twelve hours and not due off duty for another five long hours.

Yawning with tiredness and boredom he stretched his arms high then ducked under the gateway pole barrier and ambled into the middle of the deserted road. Shivering, he looked up and down the tree lined, damp cobbled road then back at the blacked out guard hut, envious of his companion he knew would be settling down for a nap.

Slinging his rifle onto his shoulder he lit a cigarette and walked to the far side of the road where he leaned against the wall and blew smoke rings into the still, damp air. Looking at his watch he became aware of a distant hum and it seemed to be quickly getting closer and louder. Recognising the sound of a jeep being driven hard, he stood up and flicked his cigarette butt away, just in time to see the faint glimmer of blacked out headlights at the end of the road heading towards him.

He ran across the road, ducked under the barrier and hammered on the guard hut door. His urgent "*Get out here now*!" was met by a slow, muffled "*What's up?*" It was too late, the jeep slewed to a halt with its front under the barrier, steam rising slowly from the tyres and as the sailor ducked to see the driver under the canvas top he recognised his commanding officer, Lieutenant Commander Virgil Korns.

"*Identity please sir*" he asked, "*Here*" was the reply and only glancing at it he had to quickly raise the barrier as Korns had already engaged gear and revving the engine lunged forward, down the drive to the steps of Hamoaze House, totally ignoring the sailor's salute.

Standing in the middle of the gateway, coughing in the cloud of exhaust smoke the sailor was joined by his buddy who asked "*Who the hell was that?*" His rather shaky answer was "*The boss, never seen him so all fired up, was in a hell of a hurry*".

Korns' desperate drive had been prompted by a telephone call only a few moments before. The loud metallic ring was exaggerated by the silent peace of his room where he had been deep asleep after a long day of almost continuous, crucial telephone calls. These had been desperate efforts to minimise the aftershock of the catastrophe on Slapton Sands when, during the D-Day rehearsal codenamed exercise "Tiger", American soldiers had been killed by Royal Navy gunfire and their own countrymen playing the role of enemy defenders.

Fumbling in the dark for the telephone, "*Yes*" he snapped. The crackly voice said "*Headquarters sir, three ships have been sunk, many dead and missing*". Korns responded, instantly awake and alert "*On my way*" and without another word slammed down the receiver. Hastily dressing, all he could murmur over and over again was "*Christ Almighty*".

This was a disaster that Korns was half expecting but was completely taken aback by the immense proportions and wasn't sure he could cover up another tragedy so soon after yesterday's events which had been a complete surprise.

Inside the old English mansion Korn's footsteps echoed as he strode down the deserted, dimly lit corridor towards the faint sound of clattering teletype machines in the message centre. Without breaking his stride he opened the door to an almost deafening, incessant rattle from half a dozen telex machines urgently churning out rolls of encoded printed messages.

One scared looking young sailor was rushing from one machine to another tearing off pages and almost running with them to the decoding office in the corner where an overweight, harassed and sweating warrant officer with tie loosened was chain smoking as he toiled to decode a rapidly increasing mountain of messages piling into his "in" tray.

Korns strode towards him and said "*Well?*" The petty officer looked up, rose quickly from his chair and fumbled through a sea of paper on his desk selecting one message handing it to Korns. "*This one sir*". Korns snatched the sheet of paper and looked down taking only seconds to read "E Boat attack. Three ships sunk. Many casualties."

At nearly 45 years old and with over twenty years as a career navy man he had never been faced with a dilemma of these proportions. With an impeccable service background from Annapolis to a Masters in mathematics and a Naval Intelligence graduation it was small wonder he had been particularly requested by Rear Admiral John E Wilkes in September 1943 to become his chief of staff. It was an appointment Korns had been delighted to accept but here and now was wishing to God he hadn't.

Captain Virgil E. Korns
United States Navy

As Commander Landing Craft and Bases, Amphibious Forces, Europe (ComLanCrabEu) Wilkes' title included the added task of conducting joint training operations with both navy and army and responsibilities for the protection of ships and ship movements from enemy air and naval action as well as supervision of experimental stations and training areas.

Whilst Wilkes was the named commander, he knew little of the intricate detail within those responsibilities, confidently leaving them to his personal choice of Chief of Staff who had the power and authority to influence all exercises and rehearsals without supervision or hindrance.

These privileges stayed with Korns when Wilkes was replaced by U.S. Navy Admiral John L. HALL in January 1944 and who's almost simultaneous appointment as commander of the U.S. Navy 11th Amphibious Force responsible for delivering the U.S. Army to their

Normandy beaches increasingly took more and more of his time. This resulted in Korns having autonomy of all matters pertaining to his commander's original role.

With access to documents of the highest security level he well knew the situation that now confronted him had been engineered at the highest level but estimates at the time of making that momentous decision did not countenance such devastation, confidently believing sufficient measures would be in place to prevent or minimise any loss.

Somehow Korns had to protect himself from the consequences of this double disaster in which his leading role could easily be tracked, secondly and for security purposes this colossal disaster had to be hushed up.

First he had to assess the scale of this disaster and with no details available he determined to make contact with those at the scene, people he could trust, those who knew when to say nothing.

Screwing the message in his hand Korns stormed out of the message centre, into the corridor and turned right, striding into the radio room where all was quiet apart from gentle tapping from half a dozen morse keys. He noticed all sailors listening with headphones shared the same puzzled and worried expression.

Immediately he entered he was confronted by the supervising petty officer who started "*There's something not right here sir ...* " but was cut short by Korns almost spitting out "*Get me Commander Tompkins on "Bayfield" – now* !"

Churning over in Korn's mind – what was he going to do about these sunken ships. There were bound to be heavy casualties, ships had been lost and shipping was critical to the invasion plan only a few weeks ahead so this loss of men and ships was catastrophic.

The highest authorities would soon be demanding answers swiftly followed by their inevitable witch hunt for scapegoats. He had to find answers fast and simultaneously distance himself from his involvement.

This was all too much. How could this have happened within hours of that stupid disaster on the beach. Korns blamed Admiral Moon for that and although the army had reacted quickly in disposing of the dead, his superiors would look at total casualties from Exercise "Tiger" regardless of which day they occurred or how they had died.

But how many had died in this double tragedy ?

Origins of "749"

THE figure of 749 that so many cling to as the definitive number of casualties of Exercise "Tiger" was calculated only a few hours after the German E-boat attack on 28th April 1944 when a lack of accurate information balanced against an urgent demand by higher command for facts produced "best guess" numbers to be seized upon.

Confusion is obvious and understandable but the earnest desire to produce a definitive number resulted in figures based on guesswork, artful calculation and deliberate misinformation rather than solid facts.

Barely twenty four hours after the sinking of two LSTs by German E-Boats, casualties were initially estimated between 300 and 400.

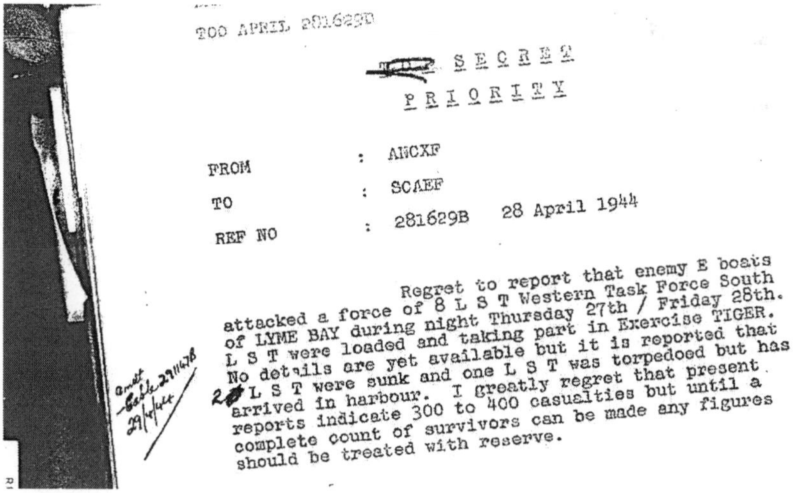
TOO APRIL 281629B

~~TOP~~ SECRET

PRIORITY

FROM : ANCXF

TO : SCAEF

REF NO : 281629B 28 April 1944

Regret to report that enemy E boats attacked a force of 8 L S T Western Task Force South of LYME BAY during night Thursday 27th / Friday 28th. L S T were loaded and taking part in Exercise TIGER. No details are yet available but it is reported that 2 L S T were sunk and one L S T was torpedoed but has arrived in harbour. I greatly regret that present reports indicate 300 to 400 casualties but until a complete count of survivors can be made any figures should be treated with reserve.

Sent by Allied Naval Commander Expeditionary Force, Admiral Sir Bertram Ramsey to the Supreme Commander Allied Expeditionary

Force, General Dwight Eisenhower, the staff officer preparing the message clearly wasn't in possession of all the facts as the message quotes eight (8) LSTs were in the attacked convoy when in fact LST 508 didn't sail so there were only seven (7), and quotes three (3) LSTs were sunk when in fact only two (LSTs 507 and 531) were sunk and LST 289 severely damaged. The content of this message suggests the author had no accurate information and was plagiarising information contained within the U.S. Navy Operation Order 2-44 for Exercise "Tiger".

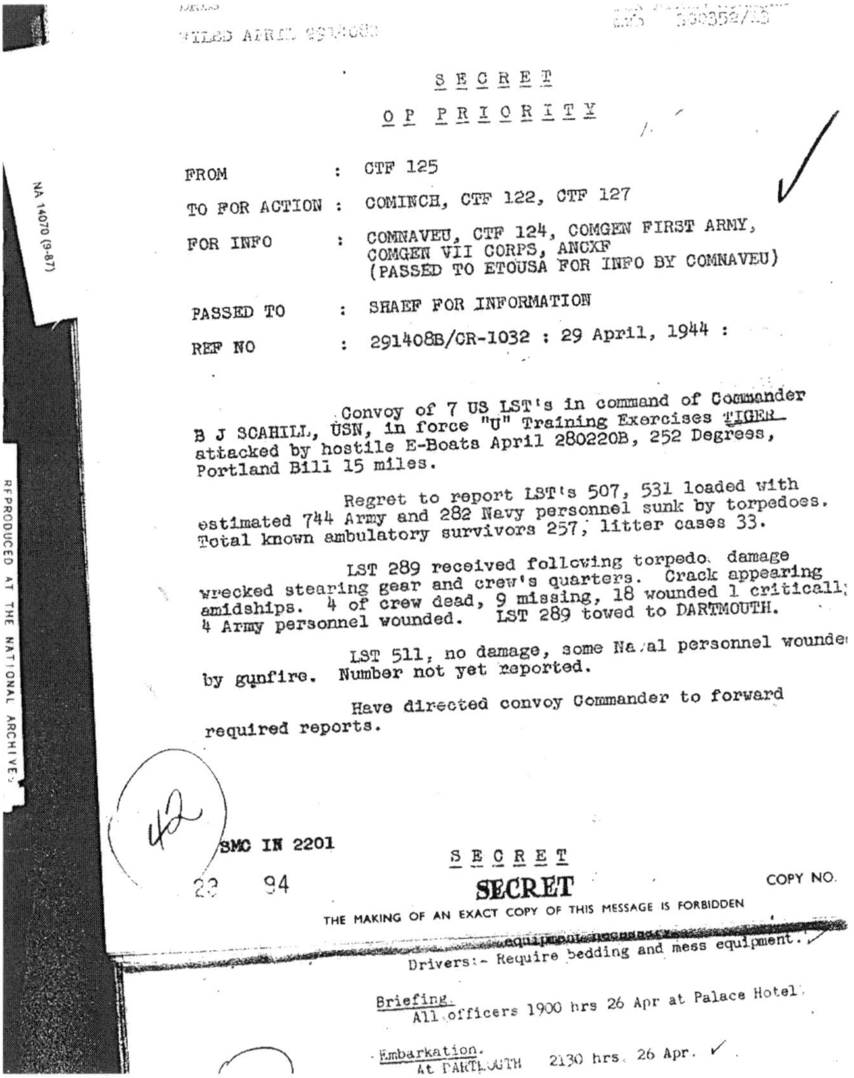

S E C R E T

O P P R I O R I T Y

FROM	:	CTF 125
TO FOR ACTION	:	COMINCH, CTF 122, CTF 127
FOR INFO	:	COMNAVEU, CTF 124, COMGEN FIRST ARMY, COMGEN VII CORPS, ANCXF (PASSED TO ETOUSA FOR INFO BY COMNAVEU)
PASSED TO	:	SHAEF FOR INFORMATION
REF NO	:	291408B/CR-1032 : 29 April, 1944 :

Convoy of 7 US LST's in command of Commander B J SCAHILL, USN, in force "U" Training Exercises TIGER attacked by hostile E-Boats April 280220B, 252 Degrees, Portland Bill 15 miles.

Regret to report LST's 507, 531 loaded with estimated 744 Army and 282 Navy personnel sunk by torpedoes. Total known ambulatory survivors 257, litter cases 33.

LST 289 received following torpedo damage wrecked stearing gear and crew's quarters. Crack appearing amidships. 4 of crew dead, 9 missing, 18 wounded 1 criticall; 4 Army personnel wounded. LST 289 towed to DARTMOUTH.

LST 511, no damage, some Naval personnel wounde by gunfire. Number not yet reported.

Have directed convoy Commander to forward required reports.

42

SMC IN 2201

S E C R E T

SECRET

COPY NO.

THE MAKING OF AN EXACT COPY OF THIS MESSAGE IS FORBIDDEN

NA 14070 (9-87)

REPRODUCED AT THE NATIONAL ARCHIVES

Drivers:- Require bedding and mess equipment.

Briefing.
All officers 1900 hrs 26 Apr at Palace Hotel.

Embarkation.
At DARTMOUTH 2130 hrs. 26 Apr.

In the hours immediately after the attack casualty numbers were fluctuating all the time – until late on 29th April 1944 when Colonel THRASHER of Southern Base Section felt confident enough to advise ETOUSA (European Theater of United States Army) Chief of Staff, Lieutenant General Walter Bedell Smith known as Eisenhower's "hatchet man", of his appraisal of the situation as 248 killed and transported to Brookwood military cemetery with 316 walking and hospitalised wounded. Thrasher's report was based upon information supplied by his units at Brookwood cemetery and Dorchester's 228th Station Hospital. The contents were repeated to the Combined Chiefs of Staff by Bedell Smith.

Earlier that same day Admiral MOON had sent his own version where his arithmetic showed 744 soldiers plus 282 sailors aboard the sunken LSTs 507 and 531 equalled 1,026. He subtracted the number of survivors at 290 reaching a sub-total of 736 before adding 13 killed or missing from the damaged LST 289 reaching his figure of 749.

MOON's report resulting in a total of 749 includes U.S. Navy casualties but the U.S. military insists 749 are all army casualties. It is known and proven there were 198 naval casualties so the result of MOON's calculations is that there are 551 army casualties. Only 447 have been positively identified from official records leaving 104 soldiers that cannot be accounted for by Admiral Moon or official records.

If the military's insisted figure of 749 is correct then navy casualties must be added making a new total of 947. Similarly, if only 447 army casualties can be identified from the suggested total of 749 then 302 soldiers are unaccounted for.

Moon may have known the true casualty figure and to minimise personal blame considered it wise and diplomatic to stick with the original estimate, or he was being fed deliberately or otherwise, inaccurate information by his subordinates or, nobody really knew.

It is interesting to note that this along with many contemporary and subsequent official calculations show a dependency upon survivors in their arithmetic to achieve a total number of casualties. One U.S. sailor and his whole landing craft crew were puzzled when ordered to write home immediately after Exercise "Tiger" telling their families they were safe and well despite neither they nor their vessel participating in the exercise. Months previously their vessel had been transported across the Atlantic to England aboard LST 507 that was sunk during the German E-Boat attack so they were classed as "survivors" of that sunken LST.

News of the tragedy couldn't be suppressed indefinitely. Casualties' families expected regular mail from their loved ones serving abroad and any unexplained cessation would provoke awkward questions that couldn't be stalled indefinitely.

The embargo on releasing names of fatalities was held firm until breaking point on 10th May 1944 when General A.D. Surles, Chief of the Bureau of Public Relations cabled the Adjutant General, War Department "*Relatives of 200 Army personnel are being notified of casualty status, most of them being missing, wounded or dead near ENGLAND 28 April*".

He further suggested "*limited announcement of ships lost and total of personnel dead or missing would remove prospective pressure for information or undue comment*".

Estimates of army casualties circulating at this date were running at around 400 so Surles' action of notifying only 200 families was minimising the number of casualties illustrating higher command's fear of revealing the truth. This also left a convenient swathe of numbers that could be later date adjusted to suit whatever official explanation was selected.

Within twenty four hours Eisenhower approved a message instructing Surles "*Supreme Headquarters strongly recommends against release at this time of information concerning ships lost and casualties sustained 28 April 1944 for security reasons*". Fear of exposing the scale of the Tiger disaster was therefore conveniently negated by the plausible excuse "*for security reasons*".

Earnest Dale RODMAN a veteran of the U.S. Army's 33rd Chemical Decontamination Company and survivor of LST 507's sinking pursued the truth for decades. In doing so he corresponded with Charles B MacDonald, a respected WWII historian who wrote and confirmed that "*749 lost is for Army personnel alone and does not include the 197 seamen lost* ".

This semi-official statement that the Navy suffered 198 casualties has been confirmed as correct according to archive records, therefore the number of army casualties of 749 may for the moment also be considered correct.

All official archive sources are adamant that army casualties amount to 749 although they can only produce evidence showing 447 soldiers casualties confirming that 302 soldiers perished during Exercise Tiger.

If these 302 didn't die within convoy T-4 when it was attacked by the Germans, they must have died during another part of this exercise, which has now been identified as the initial beach assault on 27th April 1944.

Official casualty numbers

ISOLATED in Plymouth Korns had to learn just how many casualties there were of the German E-Boat attack. His instant reaction to the news of large numbers of casualties was to immediately pull a cloak of secrecy over the affair until he was able to assess the scale of the problem. To do this he ordered U.S. Navy Captain Rutledge B. Tompkins, Admiral Moon's Chief of Staff aboard the USS "Bayfield" not only to find facts so he could analyse the probable results but also to immediately visit the captain of each LST in convoy T-4 and order them into silence.

An artful web of deceit has been woven around the casualties of Exercise "Tiger" and R. Scott MOORE, Chief, Field Programs and Historical Services of the U.S. Army Center of Military History is correct by stating that "*no attempt has been made since to minimize casualties*", since he cannot escape the figure of 749 the deception arises over who those casualties were, how they became casualties, and what happened to their bodies.

The word "casualty" is problematical as it can mean killed, missing, injured or wounded and further complicated by the sub-labels "Non battle death", "Finding of death", "Died of injuries" and "Died of wounds", all of which are classed as casualties.

In the same 2012 email from R. Scott MOORE he does confirm two important statistics ... "*It should be clearly noted that these (749) are solely Army casualty figures based on reporting from the units involved at the time ... as well as 300 wounded* ". This statement therefore confirms that wounded Army personnel are not included in their casualty figure of 749, they are all killed or missing.

It is interesting that he states that figure is based upon "*reporting from the units involved at the time*" which have to be Morning Reports and After Action Reports. All have been searched and their casualty totals do not even approach the figure of 749.

Most units suffering casualties from the German attack have comprehensive if somewhat understandably confused details of personnel killed and missing but those for the infantry units involved are blank suggesting they have been deliberately left without detail.

In paragraph "b" of a memorandum dated 24th May 1984 Alfred M. BECK, Acting Chief, Research and Analysis Division of the Center of Military History, Washington, U.S.A. reassures General KINNARD that the total number of casualties is 749.*"The total number of dead, both from enemy detonations and subsequent drownings, amounted to 749, with the possibility that many deaths were caused by indiscriminate fire from gun crews on the American vessels. Much has been made of the fact that this figure is considerably higher than the number of dead that the same units suffered in the actual assault at UTAH beach: 210"*.

BECK's statement of 210 D-Day casualties doesn't compute either because two units, the 557th QM Railhead Company and the 3206th QM Service Company that participated in Exercise "Tiger" were so badly depleted they were replaced in the assault plan and didn't take part in the Normandy landings.

Therefore his figure of 210 "Utah" casualties rests with the only other units participating in both events, being 531st Engineer Shore Regiment with their attached units, and the 4th Division infantry regiments.

Careful research shows the total casualties on 6th June 1944 on "Utah" beach is 251 which includes airborne troops and navy yet BECK does not include either in his calculation of 210 so his figure can only refer to infantry and engineers involved both in Exercise "Tiger" and the initial assault waves of D-Day.

531st Engineer Shore Regiment have fairly accurately recorded their Exercise "Tiger" and D-Day casualties which focusses attention upon the 8th Infantry Regiment which landed in the first waves upon Slapton Sands and some were loaded from LST 508 onto LST 507.

Dates of death

U.S. NAVY personnel have been treated in a puzzling manner. The vast majority of those missing in action have been awarded the "Purple Heart" yet very few wounded and even fewer killed in action received that decoration to which they are automatically entitled.

It is unexplained why some USN and USNR personnel "Missing in action" are shown as being missing on 28th April 1944 yet others are shown as missing on 29th April 1945.

The latter date may be attributed to standard military criteria of waiting for a year and a day before officially declaring them "missing" or applying a "Finding of death" but both dates appear against names in American Battle Monuments Commission cemeteries in both Normandy and Cambridge.

Equally strange and again unexplained is that some USN and USNR "MiA" are commemorated at the ABMC cemetery in Normandy while others are listed at the ABMC cemetery at Cambridge. Those MiAs commemorated in Normandy only reach the letter "H" by surname with none beyond that letter.

Casualty transport

BODIES and the few exhausted survivors trawled from the sea were collected by Royal Navy and U.S. Navy ships sent to search for them just after dawn on 28th April 1944.

To the disgust of British seamen some craft were inexplicably ordered to leave bodies in the water or cut off dog tags for identification and return those bodies to the water.

Harold Miller a crew member of Royal Navy MTB 704 searching Lyme Bay for survivors early on 28th April "*an empty personnel landing craft was sighted ... about 20 men could be seen (in the water). About 7 of them had badly sliced heads, presumably from E Boat props. Instructions were given to haul the corpses alongside and cut their ID tags but to leave them in the water*".

Corpses already retrieved were taken to Portland and unloaded on the quayside into ambulances that took them to the U.S. 50th Field Hospital tents where they were identified, personal effects removed and left on stretchers for transportation.

According to 1st Lieutenant John D. Brown, the 605th Graves Registration Company's unit historian's official version of events show his unit "*was called to process the bodies removed from two LST ships torpedoed by the enemy while on exercise in the English Channel. 262 bodies arrived in one night*".

Rodney Russell was a squad sergeant in the first platoon of the 605th Graves Registration Company stationed at Banbury, Oxfordshire, commanded by Captain William C. Bearfield. "*He went ahead and I was to load up and bring the rest of the platoon. It was dark when I reached Portland at a field hospital. Captain Bearfield told me that there had been a bombing raid and that about 300 bodies had been brought in and we had to get our job done before day break. As we began to process the bodies we found them wet, some with life vests on, so we knew the disaster happened on water. As more bodies were brought in by medical people, they told us that some LST's had been sunk".*

"It was dark and the bodies were in tents (like Hospital tents) and there were buildings on each side. We were working under black-out conditions, so the only lights available were gas lanterns on the inside of the tents and flash lights on the outside. It was light the next morning when we left and I was under the impression that the buildings on each side were being used as a hospital".

Wayne Starnes was also with the 605th Graves Registration Company, stationed at Tiverton, Devon, and was *"notified to pack and get ready to go on a mission. We were not told where we were going or why. We left headquarters about 4 or 5 pm and arrived about 9 o'clock at a hillside near the English Channel. There were several Hospital Field Tents set up at this location. After we were briefed and told of our mission, we found under the tents bodies of men who had been lost in a field operation. The men had been taken out of the water and placed in an orderly manner on stretchers with heads to the centre of the tent in two rows. Most of the bodies' clothes were still wet or damp".*

"We had to work by gas lanterns and about the time we got started German planes came over, we turned out the lights and waited for an all clear before getting back to work – we worked all night until day light. I had two or three men working with me locating dog tags and helping with identification, listing personal effects and securing the information on each body".

Night rain on 27th April 1944 gently fell on a collection of tents and trucks pitched either side of an English country lane beneath a copse of large Elm and Oak trees just east of the road between Dorchester and Portland. The lone sentry with upturned collar, wet through from hours walking the encampment in soaking rain leant against the rear of a truck and in spite of blackout regulations lit a forbidden cigarette hiding the glow between his hands.

Nothing had happened since his buddies turned in to sleep a couple of hours ago and the only sounds in the darkness were constant drips of rain from the trees and occasional snoring from the tents. There was also the very occasional hum of a vehicle passing along the main road hidden from view by a high railway embankment and bridge.

Unusually the sound of one passing vehicle on the main road changed note and the sentry saw a faint glimmer of light reflected on the wet, shiny wall under the railway bridge, yes, it was a vehicle approaching. Discarding his cigarette underfoot he stepped onto the lane and levelled his rifle ready to challenge but he recognised the sound of a jeep and discarded the idea of the enemy approaching, more likely to be some interfering officer checking the blackout and his alertness.

The jeep halted in front of him, water dripping from the canvas roof and steam rising from the hot exhaust as he moved to the driver's side to demand identification but as the canvas door opened an army officer leant across in front of the driver and asked "Where's your commanding officer ?"

A few moments later Second Lieutenant Bill Albright was being roused from sleep by the dripping wet sentry and " *introduced to a Quartermaster Corps Major wearing the general Staff metal collar insignia of SHAEF headquarters staff*".

"He enquired about my officer's training and about our unit's performance in the Middle East theatre. He stated that our unit had been selected to perform a secret "hush-hush" assignment, and that he was selecting me as the convoy commander, and he held me accountable for preserving the secrecy of the operation as far as company officers and men involved in the operation were concerned".

Bill shouted for the sentry who was hovering just outside his tent trying to listen to the conversation inside, telling him to rouse the entire unit and to send Sergeant Louis Brienza to him.

As the sentry ran off into the rain the SHAEF Major explained more of the background to Bill Albright's mission. *"The reason for secrecy is to insure good relations between the American and British allies, despite the German E-boats being able to attack the convoy because a British Royal Navy destroyer had abandoned its post and assignment to protect the exercise without being properly relieved by an American destroyer. As a result the British and American naval staff attached to SHAEF were at each other's throats over the incident. The decision to keep the incident secret was to avoid bickering at military staff levels, and also to avoid publicising the incident for consumption by British and American military and civilians. The secrecy decision was a correct one, for no amount of finger-pointing could change the disastrous result, and harmony between the Allies is most important in the crucial months which lay ahead".*

Within an hour the 146th Quartermaster Truck Company had activated all operational vehicles, and did a shake down to ensure that all vehicles were equipped with their side stakes, bows, tarpaulin covers and rear tarpaulin curtains.

Leaving at about 2.00 am and driving with blackout lights, forty 6-wheeled trucks and Lieutenant Albright's jeep followed the major to Weymouth.

Arriving at Portland Sergeant Louis Brienza was told that "*we were going to transport dead soldiers to an American cemetery near London. The dead soldiers had been in a training exercise in the English Channel when they were attacked by German E-boats. All their craft were destroyed and all the soldiers who were in the water were shot by the Germans. Then the U.S. Army or the U.S. Navy picked them up and took them to a place near Weymouth where they were cleaned up and identified*".

One of the 146th' drivers Rudy Weber arrived at Portland when "*it was still dark and there was a strange smell in the air. When we asked about it some soldier told us to look into some very large tents. These tents were very long and when I looked in I saw row on row of dead wrapped in blankets on stretchers. We were told that troops on LSTs were on landing exercises and some German E-boats snuck in and sank some of them then machine-gunned the men in the water*".

This was a rumour embellished as it passed from soldier to soldier but when the 605th Graves Registration platoon completed their task just before dawn, they had found that although some of the bodies were missing arms and legs, they had seen nothing that resembled bullet wounds.

Although Wayne Starnes had "*talked with some of the survivors at chow the morning before leaving, one stated that he was in the 40 degree water for some time. He stated that some of the German E-Boats came back and made a pass at them and fired on the ones in the water*".

Shortly after dawn Rodney Russell and his Graves Registration colleagues finished their work and stood silently together outside the tents, stretching their aching backs after hours of working bent over the rows of corpses, removing and bagging their personal possessions, listing them, checking "dog tags" and completing identification forms.

"*Captain Bearfield said there were about 300 bodies when I arrived and I know more were brought in all through the night*".

"It became my job to see that the trucks were loaded. I loaded twelve bodies on each truck; six on the floor and six on the seats after they were turned down. The tarpaulin tops were tied down so that no one could see what was inside. A First Lieutenant was able to find a hole where he could see a foot and he chewed me out. I am sure that there were twelve bodies on each truck and I think about forty trucks".

The trucks were loaded under Bill Albright's supervision "*with seven litters placed upon the truck bed floor and six litters resting on the truck bed sides, providing transport for thirteen bodies per truck*".

Rudy Weber watched the trucks being loaded "*two tiers high with a rope down the centre, over the bodies to prevent them from bouncing off the stretchers. A blanket was used as a curtain at the second last bow and a soldier from the Graves Registration in Class One uniform with a rifle sat at the back of each truck as Honor Guard*".

When all trucks in the convoy had been loaded and checked, all personnel involved, Graves Registration; Medical and the drivers were called alongside the trucks. Rodney Russell remembers "*We were given a long talk by a First Lieutenant who was an Adjutant from General Eisenhower's office about not letting the enemy know how bad we had been hit. He told us we would be going as a guarded convoy to Brookwood and that any man would be court-martialled if he ever talked about what was on those trucks. He said if someone asked to just say, "we don't talk about it"*.

An order the 146th' drivers obeyed for over sixty years.

Before returning to their trucks the 146th drivers were called over by Bill Albright who repeated the order "*You will not communicate with civilians or any military personnel, other than our personnel serving on the assignment. We will be running non-stop and escorted by a Military Police motorcycle escort*".

Trucks started their engines and began following the lead motorcyclist. Rudy Weber says "*It was a large convoy, run with tight spacing and it was difficult driving because the speed chosen forced you to shift gears constantly – too slow for one gear and too fast for the next. The MPs patrolled the convoy to keep other traffic out and there was also an MP at each and every intersection on the route to ensure that no truck had to stop.*

"At the end of the trip they told us that ours was the best convoy they ever saw – I remember thinking that these dead deserved it".

Wayne Starnes, Lieutenant Carlson his platoon leader, and the jeep driver led the convoy out of Portland "*loaded with 527 bodies going to Brookwood Military Cemetery*".

Garland Coghill followed Rudy's truck with "*Thirteen bodies on my truck, I remember looking at these young boys and it seemed like they were just sleeping with their uniforms and shoes on. Going through towns and villages – seemed very early in the morning – I could see people looking up at the backs of the trucks expecting to see troops or something. All the tarpaulins were closed so they couldn't see anything and we'd see an odd expression on their faces*".

The convoy arrived at Brookwood cemetery on a warm, sunlit day to be met by Graves Registration personnel who had been waiting for them. Litters were unloaded truck by truck allowing time for the 146th drivers to wander around the cemetery.

Alone, Rudy Weber came across "*a small brick building. Inside was a coffin being made ready for burial and it seemed that this pilot was shot down over the Channel and had been in the water for about a month. No head, just some skin and bones. Sawdust was put in the civilian type coffin and the remains placed on top. On top of this was his uniform. Shirt sleeves in jacket sleeves, shirt tail in trousers, tie tied around shirt collar – just like a man when dressed, with his dog tags pinned to the lapel. This entire experience left me with great respect for the way the services treated their dead*".

Fred Cox walked quietly with another small group around the cemetery and came across a small building. "*We looked in the windows and saw the bodies lying on the tables dressed in green fatigue uniforms. While looking at the bodies that lay on the tables, I was impressed by the fact that there were no signs of injuries. But for the pallor of their faces and hands, they could have been asleep. On their left (uniform) shoulders they wore a medium blue rectangular patch embossed with a golden anchor. I had heard this patch signified "Combined Operations"*.

Their task completed the 146th headed back to Dorchester leaving the Graves Registration personnel who had accompanied their convoy at Brookwood for about five more days to assist personnel already there to dress all the victims in Class A uniforms and bury them in individual graves.

Less than 24 hours later Colonel THRASHER of U.S. Army Southern Base Section reported that 248 bodies had been transported to Brookwood.

Despite the most meticulous work by graves registration personnel at Portland they were unable to fully identify every body before the convoy departed. On 29th April 1944 the 625th Ordnance Ammunition Company despatched First Lieutenant Marvin E. Shaw and Staff Sergeant Raymond H. Lather to Brookwood to attempt to identify any of their unit not knowing at that time that 10 were missing and 2 had been killed.

Burial at Brookwood

QUARTER Master Corps Form No.2 GRS was a weekly summary of all burials of American service personnel compiled from Graves Registration Service reports from emergency and temporary cemeteries. They detailed casualties' name, service number, rank, unit and date of burial.

Brookwood burial sheets show a total of 151 Army and 117 Navy burials from Exercise "Tiger" between 1st and 4th May 1944. This total of 268 roughly equates with Colonel THRASHER's figure of 248 but represents only half that of the 146th QM Truck Company and Graves Registration's count, and both units were fastidious about the accuracy of their loads.

Mistakes within these burial sheets are common often showing incorrect service numbers and mis-spelling of names which may be attributed to illiteracy or innumeracy of staff preparing these lists, or a clumsy attempt at deception.

A notable example of inaccuracy among these burial sheets is the absence of a sailor, Walter Humphris FRAZIER. Other records show that he was indeed buried at Brookwood after an initial report of him being missing from LST 289. His "missing" status is confirmed by that ship's muster roll of 30th April 1944, but according to the official U.S. Navy casualty report he is buried at Arlington cemetery where his headstone gives a date of death as 29th April 1945. This date a year and a day after Exercise Tiger confirms he is indeed "Missing" and the headstone is only a memorial. But the American Battle Monuments Commission who list all those missing in action have no record of FRAZIER as dead or missing.

The conclusion is that another casualty was identified as FRAZIER and buried at Brookwood but that body's true identity and final resting

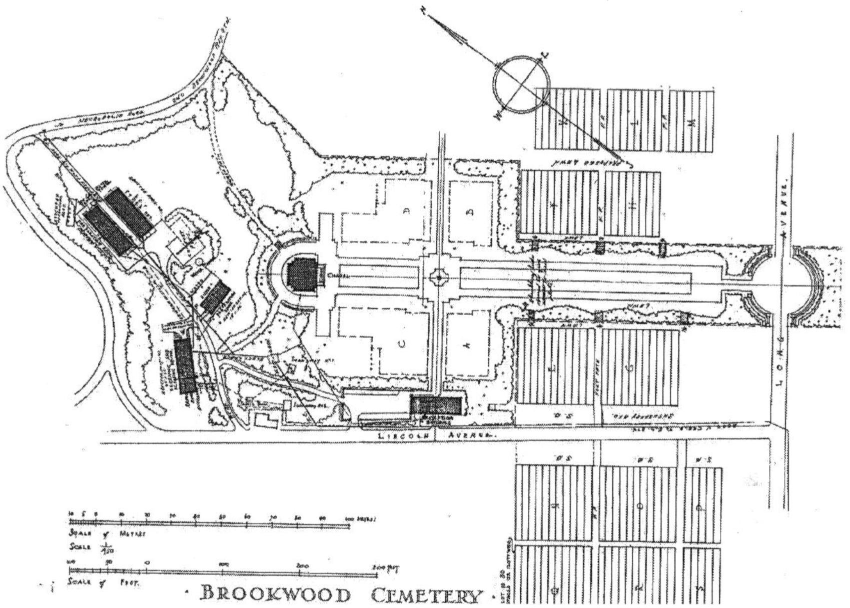

place is unknown. At Brookwood most bodies were buried in Block "R" which was dedicated to "Tiger" casualties with a few in adjoining Block "Q" alongside casualties of other units who died in that same time period at the end of April 1944.

The 1st Engineer Special Brigade list of casualties compared against Brookwood burial sheets highlight two names. Both are shown on the 1st ESB list as casualties of Exercise "Tiger" yet not buried at Brookwood, instead both are shown as being buried in Normandy.

Robert P. Motley, Private, 33042113 of the 557th QM Railhead Company was initially buried at Saint Andre de l'Epine, France (military code 3572) in grave J-9-169 before his body was transferred to the ABMC cemetery at St. Laurent sur Mer, Normandy.

It has been meekly suggested by a U.S. archive source that Motley's body drifted onto the French coast near Calais in August 1944, was recovered and buried at St Andre de l'Epine, near Paris.

Donald S. Bryant, Private First Class, 31097544 of the same unit was initially buried at 607 Macon emergency cemetery behind Utah beach on 8th June 1944 then reburied at Ste Mere Eglise #2 (military code 3586) temporary cemetery in Normandy on 25th June 1944 before repatriation to New York in 1948.

Both were members of a unit that didn't participate in the D-Day landings or even the Normandy campaign so they have both slipped through the cover-up net and these burial locations are suspect leading to the conclusion more "Tiger" casualties were physically buried in Normandy or given dates of death within the Normandy campaign that ran from 6th June to 25th August 1944.

Blameworthy

MOON knew, as the responsible officer for the planning and execution of Exercise "Tiger", there would be terrible retribution for this catastrophic loss of life and shipping that threatened Operation Neptune only a few short weeks ahead and he started to hint where the blame lay. Firstly he named U.S. Navy Commander B.J. SCAHILL as commander of the ill-fated convoy T-4 having ultimate responsibility which was probably prompted by SCAHILL's disobedience to MOON's orders not to return to the attack area in his vessel (LST 515) and pick up survivors.

On 30th April 1944 following his prickly meeting with Royal Navy Admiral Leatham, Moon submitted a further report in an attempt to spread the blame even further, this time outlining the mistakes and shortcomings of Royal Navy Plymouth Command in failing to adequately protect his convoy.

This was disputed by Royal Navy Admiral Sir Ralph Leatham who wriggled from blame by quoting extracts from a letter he had written on 1st January 1944 to U.S. Navy Admiral HALL after confusion of responsibilities had arisen during previous American exercises with Royal Navy protection.

Within this letter LEATHAM passed tactical control of American and Royal Navy vessels from the point of departure to the exercise area to the U.S. naval officer in charge of the exercise, but LEATHAM retained control of covering forces which in the case of Exercise "Tiger" consisted of several elderly destroyers and five Motor Torpedo Boats.

Moon could not deny he was responsible for delaying H-Hour on 27th April 1944 and can be held accountable for that message not reaching every vessel resulting in the beach bombardment while

American troops were landing with subsequent losses. But MOON was in an invidious position, he knew from the highest authority his convoy would most probably be attacked but national security prevented him from revealing this to those who may have successfully countered it.

Someone had to take the blame for this loss of life and shipping and immediately after the exercise General Omar N. Bradley, commander of American ground forces in the upcoming Normandy invasion discussed this with his staff officers KEANE, THORSON, DICKSON and WILSON. Moon couldn't be seen to be responsible as he was taking the "Utah" force to Normandy and another force to invade the south of France. There was no time to replace him and if it was made known he was responsible for the disaster, the effect upon morale of the entire invasion forces would be catastrophic.

A scapegoat had to be found and Bradley concluded "*The beach engineer organization had broken down*" and therefore recommended to Major General J. Lawton COLLINS, VII Corps Commander that ... "*he assign a new commander to the Utah Beach engineer brigade*".

This resulted in Colonel Eugene M. CAFFEY being relieved of his command of the 1st Engineer Special Brigade and replaced by his deputy. COLLINS was well aware that CAFFEY had been done a cruel injustice and retained him as deputy commander, effectively still in command.

Bribery for silence was common practice for many of those involved in the aftermath of Exercise "Tiger" who were promoted, posted upwards or awarded some medal or decoration. Some survivors including Dale RODMAN received the French Croix de Guerre, most received the Purple Heart even if they had not been wounded or injured and hospital lists were falsified accordingly.

All participants were informed of a VII Corps memorandum ordering no discussion of the event with anyone not involved in the exercise, some interpreting any transgression would result in court martial.

Brookwood burial sheets true, false, altered or re-written were all signed off on behalf of Colonel Allen R. KIMBALL, Deputy Chief Quartermaster who after Exercise "Tiger" was promoted to Brigadier General, and on 26th August 1944 held the post of ETO Headquarters Commandant.

RESTRICTED

HEADQUARTERS VII CORPS

SHEPLEGH COURT
29 April 1944

MEMORANDUM:

TO : Commanding General or Commanding Officer of Units Participating in the Exercise.

Regarding enemy activity of night 27 – 28 April during the exercise, members of this command will not mention the incident to military personnel not participating in the exercise nor to civilians either orally or in writing until authorized by this headquarters. Advise all concerned.

By command of Major General COLLINS:

R. G. McKEE,
Colonel, GSC,
Chief of Staff.

DISTRIBUTION:
"Special"

Kimball was awarded a Bronze Star with Oak Leaf cluster, Legion of Merit with Oak Leaf cluster and Croix de Guerre with Palm and by May 1945 had been moved to the Pacific Theatre of Operations where during an interview made an astonishing quote … "*Plan for what you want in the future and don't try to do it by hidden figures*".

Commander Virgil Eben KORNS, U.S. Navy was the true architect of the naval element of Exercise "Tiger" and he too was richly rewarded with promotion, high honours and awards before his eventual posting to the Pacific theatre of operations.

He inherited Admiral Wilkes' job as Commander of US Amphibious Bases in the United KIngdom commanding 1,500 officers and 30,000 men and was awarded the British OBE … "*for high endeavor and most successful co-operation in matters concerning the mutual naval interests of the USA and the UK in the Plymouth Command, first as Chief of Staff and later as Commander, US Amphibious Bases, UK*".

In July 1944 he was awarded the Legion of Merit by the Commander, US Naval Forces in Europe. Less than a year later he received a Gold Star in lieu of a second Legion of Merit for his work in connection with "*replacing vessels lost in the storm off Omaha beach*" in mid June 1944. Over the next few months he was awarded several more high status medals including the French Legion of Honor, the French

Croix de Guerre with Palm, the Belgian Order of Leopold and Croix de Guerre.

Someone far senior to Korns knew what he had done in shielding his superior officers, and ensured he was handsomely rewarded for a job well done – and to safeguard his continuing silence.

Cover up

KORNS knew the size of the cover-up was going to be immense and complicated, especially once he heard the scale of casualties but he was confident of complete co-operation and support from those at the very highest levels. Especially those who knew the Germans had been tipped off as they bore ultimate responsibility for the situation and would be keen to divest themselves of any blame and to hide the truth.

Tasked with clearing up their mess, with mathematical precision and in ordered sequence he formed a list of the complex tasks ahead that had to be achieved in complete secrecy. The alteration, falsification or destruction of relevant documents, maintaining the silence of all survivors, and scapegoats had to be found.

He had to co-ordinate actions and relied upon fear of personal exposure to blame to gain the co-operation of those who knew of the secret tip-off and he wasn't averse to manipulating senior officers.

Initially his main target was Admiral Moon as naval commander of Exercise "Tiger" and Korns used U.S. Navy Captain M. T. Richardson, commander of the "Green" assault group to brief Admiral Moon in a meeting aboard the USS Bayfield in the morning of 29th April 1944 as to what was expected of him. Here Moon was presented with casualty figures he was to quote in his report later that day.

Late in the morning of 28th April 1944 Moon had signalled that naval participation in Exercise "Tiger" had been completed. His flagship USS Bayfield departed Slapton Sands and anchored in Plymouth Sound at 5.03 pm when Moon immediately left for a meeting with British Admiral Leatham, C in C, Plymouth Command, Royal Navy, U.S. Navy Rear Admirals Kirk, Wilkes, and Struble.

Plymouth Command could sense the Americans were looking for someone to blame, and were quick to advise them of what action they had taken on the E-Boat reports.

It was now time to generate reasons for the German E-Boat success and divert attention away from the fact they left Cherbourg, evaded the Royal Navy screen, sank one of their destroyers and went straight to convoy T-4. No searching, no lucky discovery, the Germans knew exactly what they were looking for and where it would be found.

Suggestions of increased radio traffic attracting German radio direction finding stations was one idea. Blaming a typographical error of radio frequencies within the operational order was another.

But Royal Navy Plymouth Command had indeed relayed E-Boat reports on the agreed "Port Wave" radio frequency monitored by convoy T4's lead vessel, LST 515 and these were overheard by ships of the protective screen. Radio operators aboard LST 515 would then relay any relevant information to other vessels of convoy T4 on a separate frequency.

This task was complicated by Communications Annex "LOVE" to the operational order for Exercise Tiger advising *"That bogus (radio) traffic may be expected, and will actually be introduced, for the exercise"*.

This could only be identified and challenged using four complex coded tables and it appears that LST 515 radio personnel wrongly identified the Royal Navy E-Boat warnings as "bogus" and didn't pass this information to other vessels in the convoy.

Back in Plymouth Korns' burning question was what to do with the bodies of the beach bombardment of 27th April ? They had already been buried in fields around Blackawton but he knew they couldn't stay there indefinitely as the civilian population would soon be returning to their homes and farms.

Cover-up uncovered

THE very first hint of how the deception was engineered concerning the number and unit identity of casualties comes from the burial of Donald S. BRYANT of the 557th Quartermaster Railhead Company, 531st Engineer Shore Regiment, whose unit participated in the exercise and suffered many fatalities during the German E-Boat attack.

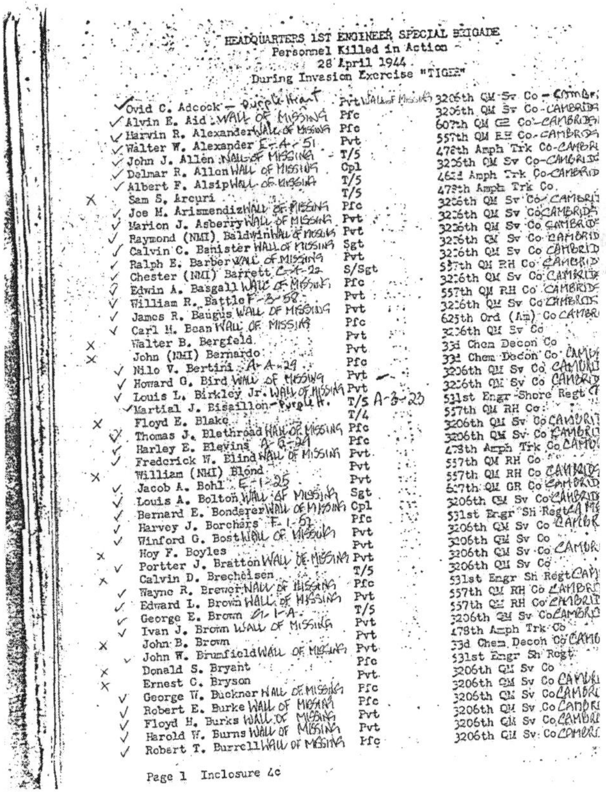

HEADQUARTERS 1ST ENGINEER SPECIAL BRIGADE
Personnel Killed in Action
28 April 1944
During Invasion Exercise "TIGER"

Ovid C. Adcock	Pvt	3206th QM Sv Co
Alvin E. Aid	Pfc	3206th QM Sv Co
Marvin R. Alexander	Pfc	607th QM GR Co
Walter W. Alexander	Pvt	557th QM RH Co
John J. Allen	T/5	478th Amph Trk Co
Delmar R. Allon	Cpl	3206th QM Sv Co
Albert F. Alsip	T/5	462d Amph Trk Co
Sam S. Arcuri	T/5	478th Amph Trk Co
Joe M. Arismendiz	Pfc	3206th QM Sv Co
Marion J. Asberry	Pvt	3206th QM Sv Co
Raymond (NMI) Baldwin	Pvt	3206th QM Sv Co
Calvin C. Banister	Sgt	3206th QM Sv Co
Ralph E. Barber	Pvt	3206th QM Sv Co
Chester (NMI) Barrett	S/Sgt	557th QM RH Co
Edwin A. Basgall	Pfc	3206th QM Sv Co
William R. Battle	Pvt	557th QM RH Co
James R. Baugus	Pvt	3206th QM Sv Co
Carl M. Bean	Pfc	625th Ord (Am) Co
Walter B. Bergfeld	Pvt	3206th QM Sv Co
John (NMI) Bernardo	Pvt	33d Chem Decon Co
Nilo V. Bertini	Pfc	33d Chem Decon Co
Howard G. Bird	Pvt	3206th QM Sv Co
Louis L. Birkley Jr.	Pvt	3206th QM Sv Co
Martial J. Bisaillon	T/5	531st Engr Shore Regt
Floyd E. Blake	T/4	557th QM RH Co
Thomas J. Blethroad	Pfc	3206th QM Sv Co
Harley E. Blevins	Pfc	3206th QM Sv Co
Frederick W. Blind	Pvt	478th Amph Trk Co
William (NMI) Blond	Pvt	557th QM RH Co
Jacob A. Bohl	Pvt	557th QM RH Co
Louis A. Bolton	Sgt	607th QM GR Co
Bernard E. Bonderer	Cpl	3206th QM Sv Co
Harvey J. Borchers	Pfc	531st Engr Sh Regt
Winford G. Bost	Pvt	3206th QM Sv Co
Hoy F. Boyles	Pvt	3206th QM Sv Co
Portter J. Bratton	Pvt	3206th QM Sv Co
Calvin D. Brecheisen	T/5	3206th QM Sv Co
Wayne R. Brewer	Pfc	531st Engr Sh Regt
Edward L. Brown	Pvt	557th QM RH Co
George E. Brown	T/5	557th QM RH Co
Ivan J. Brown	Pvt	3206th QM Sv Co
John B. Brown	Pvt	478th Amph Trk Co
John W. Brumfield	Pvt	33d Chem Decon Co
Donald S. Bryant	Pfc	531st Engr Sh Regt
Ernest C. Bryson	Pvt	3206th QM Sv Co
George W. Buckner	Pfc	3206th QM Sv Co
Robert E. Burke	Pfc	3206th QM Sv Co
Floyd H. Burks	Pvt	3206th QM Sv Co
Harold W. Burns	Pvt	3206th QM Sv Co
Robert T. Burrell	Pfc	3206th QM Sv Co

Page 1 Inclosure 4c

Listed as a fatal casualty of Exercise "Tiger" on 28th April 1944 within the 1st Engineer Special Brigade casualty report, further records show he was initially buried at temporary cemetery "607 Macon" in Normandy on 8th June 1944.

RESTRICTED

Q.C Form
No.2-GRS

314.6 Q-GRS (Trans).

SEP 11 1944

SUBJECT: Q.C Form No.2 GRS
Weekly Report of Burials. No. 99

NAME	SOLDIERS NO.	RANK	ORGANIZATION	DATE OF BURIAL Dy M. Yr	CEMETERY
2221. DE CICCO, John (NMI)	32157433	S/Sgt.	8 Inf. Regt.	8 Jun 44	607 Macon Temporary
2222. BRYANT, Donald S.	31097544	Pfc.	531 Eng Regt Sh	8 " "	"
2223. AARON, Carl J.	34779685	Pvt.	237 Eng C Bn.	9 " "	"

After reburial at Ste Mere Eglise #2, Normandy (military code 3586) on 25th June 1944, his body was repatriated to Long Island cemetery, New York in 1949 where his interment card states he was a member of the Medical Detachment, 1st Battalion, 531st Engineer Shore Regiment and his headstone shows his date of death as 6th June 1944.

4 INTERMENT IN THE LONG ISLAND CEMETERY QYA-16 ORIGINAL

TO: THE QUARTERMASTER GENERAL, WASHINGTON 25, D. C.

RELIGIOUS EMBLEM (Check One): LATIN CROSS ☐ STAR OF DAVID — AUG 9 1949

NAME (Last, first, middle initial): BRYANT, Donald S.

STATE: Mass.

RANK: Pfc.

SERIAL NO.: 31097544

SERVICE DATA (Company, regiment, or other organization or branch of service and division, if any): 531 Engr. Shore Regt U.S.A. Med Det 1st Bn WW II

DATE OF BIRTH (Month / Day / Year)	DATE OF DEATH (Month / Day / Year)	DATE OF INTERMENT (Month / Day / Year)	GRAVE LOCATION (Sec. or Plot / Grave or Lot No.)
4-23-13	6 6 44	July 14 1948	H- 8026

DATES OF SERVICE: Enlistment / Died on A. D. ✓ / Discharge / Retirement

REMARKS (Authority for interment, pension or claim number, disinterment, etc.): WW II Dead returned from St. Mere Eglise No2- Carentan

DATE HEADSTONE ORDERED AND B/L NUMBER: GREEN MOUNTAIN, VT. SEP 24 1948 3851101

SHIPPING POINT FOR HEADSTONES — RAILROAD STATION FOR FREIGHT: PINELAWN, L. I., NEW YORK

POST OFFICE ADDRESS: 315 ENCLOSED

SIGNATURE OF SUPERINTENDENT OF NATIONAL CEMETERY OR QM OF POST OR POW CEMETERY: John C. Metzler (SIGNATURE)

QMC FORM 14 REV 1 AUG 45 Previous editions may be used 9 0 F 2 0 0 1 0 0 1 9 (See instructions on reverse side) 16—65609-1

Confirmation of the method of achieving a cover-up is the disposal of another casualty under similar circumstances. Robert P. MOTLEY,

service number 33042113 of the same unit as BRYANT was initially buried at Saint Andre de l'Epine (military code 3572), conveniently with no date of burial, before re-burial within the ABMC cemetery at St. Laurent sur Mer, Normandy (military code 3505).

Motley is also listed on the 1st Engineer Special Brigade casualty report as a fatal casualty of Exercise "Tiger" on 28th April 1944.

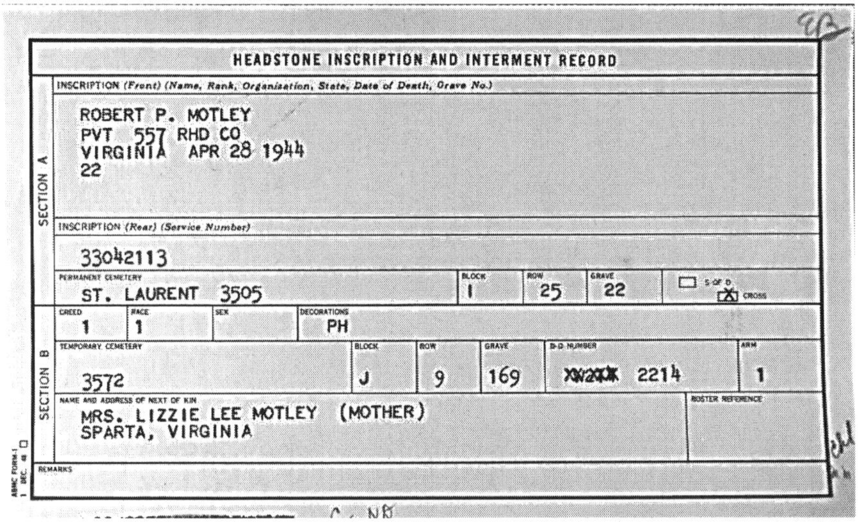

HEADSTONE INSCRIPTION AND INTERMENT RECORD

SECTION A

INSCRIPTION (Front) (Name, Rank, Organization, State, Date of Death, Grave No.)

ROBERT P. MOTLEY
PVT 557 RHD CO
VIRGINIA APR 28 1944
22

INSCRIPTION (Rear) (Service Number)

33042113

PERMANENT CEMETERY	BLOCK	ROW	GRAVE		
ST. LAURENT 3505	I	25	22	☐ S of D	☒ CROSS

SECTION B

CREED	RACE	SEX	DECORATIONS
1	1		PH

TEMPORARY CEMETERY	BLOCK	ROW	GRAVE	B-D NUMBER	ARM
3572	J	9	169	XXXXX 2214	1

NAME AND ADDRESS OF NEXT OF KIN
MRS. LIZZIE LEE MOTLEY (MOTHER)
SPARTA, VIRGINIA

ROSTER REFERENCE

REMARKS

ABMC FORM-1
1 DEC. 48

Bryant and Motley are representative of the deceitful documentary trail so carefully planned proving the lie that all bodies recovered from the German E-Boat attack were processed at Portland, England, identified and buried at Brookwood cemetery (military code 1605). Despite the discrepancy of the number of bodies between the unit that conveyed them from Portland and those buried at Brookwood.

Korns knew any cover up to alter the number of casualties would entail the falsification of documents, and with so many agencies and

X Alvin C. Morgan... Pfc
✓ Aloysius G. Morgenstern 4-5-6 Pfc
✓ Edwin F. Morse D-3-91 Pvt
✓ Robert P. Motley I-25-22 Pvt
✓ Raymond J. Murphey WALL OF MISSING Cpl
✓ Hugh C. Murray WALL OF MISSING Pfc
✓ James E. Music WALL OF MISSING Pfc
✓ Michael J. Naccarelli WALL OF MISSING Pvt
✓ Curtis A. Nagle F-3-91 Pfc
✓ Hyman (NMI) Nathan 9-7-6 Pvt
✓ Robert T. New WALL OF MISSING Pvt
✓ Aubrey L. Newman WALL OF MISSING Pfc

557th QM RH Co - CAMBRIDGE
557th QM RH Co NORMANDY —
557th QM RH Co CAMBRIDGE
320th QM Sv Co CAMBRIDGE
557th QM RH Co CAMBRIDGE
462d Amph Trk Co CAMBRIDGE
320th QM Sv Co CAMBRIDGE
557th QM RH Co CAMBRIDGE
320th QM Sv Co CAMBRIDGE
320th QM Sv Co CAMBRIDGE

Page 5 Inclosure 4c

organisations involved in handling bodies and each creating their own paper records this would be nearly impossible to manipulate or control.

During Dale RODMAN's life-long quest for true casualty numbers of Exercise "Tiger" he received one confusing and complicated document in particular which may show that truth. Sent to him in 1984 by U.S. Army Colonel BADGER, an employee of the American Battle Monuments Commission at that time, his document suggests a total casualty figure of 1,405. This document is not in the public domain and while it may show a true number of fatalities, few of the totals can be reconciled and it may be part of a larger plan to deliberately deceive and confuse those seeking the truth.

EXERCISE TIGER PERSONNEL ACCOUNTING

A	B 1ST ENG SPEC. BRIG.	C 35TH SIG. BN	D U.S. NAVY	E SUB-TOTAL	F UNSPECIFIED UNITS	G GRAND TOTAL
1 BURIED AT BROOKWOOD	142	2	34	178	82	260
2 VARIOUS SITES (REPATRIATED?)	271	17	84	372	156	528
3 BODIES RECOVERED TOTAL	413	19	118	550	238	788
4 MISSING	334	9	80	423	193	616
5 TOTAL DEAD AND MISSING	747	28	198	973	431	1405
6 RESCUED	191	4	122	317	110	427
7 TOTAL ABOARD	938	32	320	1290	542	1832

DOCUMENTATION
CELL #
B1 BRIGADE KIA PER NEPTUNE: TRANING FOR AND MOUNTING THE ATTACK, PAGE 259.BY C.L. JONES
B2 BRIGADE MIA SAME ABOVE
B3 BRIGADE TOTAL KILLED AND MISSING SAME ABOVE
C1 NON-BRIG (35TH SIG CONST BN) AT CAMBRIDGE
C2 NON-BRIG GRAVES AT CAMBRIDGE
C4 ARMY TOTAL 441 LESS 413 LESS NON-BRIG AT CAMBRIDGE 19
D1 NAVY GRAVE SITES AT CAMBRIDGE
D3 BODIES RECOVERED PER NAVY LIST OF CASUALTIES
D4 MISSING PER NAVY LIST OF CASUALTIES
G1 BURIED AT BROOKWOOD PER PASSING REVIEW PAGE 3 CHAPTER 26 BY COLO. L.R. TALBOT
C6 SIG CONST BN PER LST 531 SURVIVORS LISTY

The accuracy of this document was put to the American Battle Monuments Commission and their dismissive response from Michael

G CONLEY, Director of Public Affairs was that they "*cannot comment on the purpose or basis of a letter written by a former ABMC employee 20 years ago* ". And they introduce an element of doubt as to the accuracy of that figure of 749 " *A complete list of casualties is not available, but* ***Army records, possibly not complete****, state that 749 were killed and more than 300 either injured or suffering from severe exposures* ".

So the same number is repeated yet again, but now introducing an element of doubt as to their accuracy.

The U.S. Military History Institute hold an eight page list compiled shortly after the incident by Headquarters, 1st Engineer Special Brigade listing their casualties from sunken ships during Exercise "Tiger" totalling 413 leaving 336 soldiers unaccounted for from the accepted number of 749.

If these 336 weren't from the 1st Engineer Special Brigade there are three possibilities. They were from other units aboard another vessel that was sunk during that same attack although U.S. Navy vessel and personnel records negate this possibility. Alternatively they are from units not involved with the convoy attacked by the Germans and therefore died during the first day of the exercise, 27th April 1944 – 8th Infantry Regiment. Or they were aboard one of the sunken LSTs but not detailed on the manifest or loading sheets. The strongest possibility here is that when LST 508 was unable to sail, her personnel load including 287 of 8th Infantry Regiment was transferred to LST 507 which was subsequently sunk.

The discrepancy of over 300 soldiers unaccounted for now rests firmly upon the 8th Infantry Regiment who had personnel killed during the initial beach assault at Slapton on 27th April 1944, and personnel transferred from LST 508 to LST 507 at Brixham.

Deception

DURING World War II a U.S. Navy officer serving aboard an LST in Britain was engaged to a British WAAF radar operator and told her *"that it was general knowledge amongst the Americans, that the dead of Operation (sic) Tiger were boxed up and temporarily buried locally on the US occupied ground until such time that they could be intermingled with the dead from the (D-Day) landings and then repatriated to the US following the Invasion of D-Day, claiming that they had fallen in action"*.

Some fifty years later two British tourists began chatting with an American war veteran in the Normandy cemetery and he told them … *"that the true casualties at Slapton had never been revealed, because the American authorities did not want the people back home to know how their sons had been killed. It would have been unacceptable to the American people. They therefore added the names of men lost at Slapton Sands to the list of those men killed on the landing beaches at Utah and Omaha"*.

Lieutenant Sean DAVIS, U.S. Navy, narrated a film "Dartmouth at war" in which he states … *"More than one thousand deaths occurred as a result* (of the German E-Boat attack) *and probably more. Some deaths were originally attributed to D-Day"*.

This is anecdotal evidence of how the cover-up was implemented and investigation has proved it is correct. Casualties of Exercise Tiger who weren't buried at Brookwood are hidden amongst the dead of D-Day and the Normandy campaign as illustrated by the burial of MOTLEY and BRYANT in Normandy.

KORNS was still struggling with his damage limitation scheme. He had no problem exerting his authority and putting pressure on junior naval officers who had survived the German E-Boat attack of 28th April 1944 to write their after action reports just the way he wanted them. In a few cases he returned reports that did not conform to his version to be re-written, corrected or overseen by a senior officer to ensure conformity to the official story that was taking shape.

Ensign Douglas G. HARLANDER the senior survivor of LST 531 concluded his report of 2nd May 1944 with the line ... "*assisted by Commander B. J. SCAHILL*". SCAHILL was initially criticised and blamed by Admiral MOON but appears to have been convinced of the necessity to promote the official version of events and thereafter all blame levelled against him simply evaporates.

Documents such as loading manifests and personnel records of participating units were deemed "lost in action". Dale Rodman was told his personnel file had gone down with LST 507 but he questioned why personnel records would be taken on a live exercise. When he was discharged at war's end his complete file was in front of him.

KORNS was also astute enough to recognise his deception had to be continued for some time and selected a few naval officers already at the survivor's camp at Vicarage Road, Plymouth, to do this.

Among them were Lieutenant Eugene E. ECKSTAM a medical officer aboard LST 507 and Lieutenant James MURDOCK senior survivor of LST 507.

Vicarage Road Camp, Plymouth, May 1944: Back Row, Left to Right: Ensigns Alexander Z "Jerry" Brown (507), Thomas F. Clark (507), Frederick O. Beattie (507), Dr. Edward G. Panter (507), Lt. James F. Murdock (507), Dr. Eugene E. Eckstam (507)

Both were returned to the United States in August 1944 for "survivor leave". ECKSTAM was being shipped away to the Pacific Theatre of Operations and took the opportunity to promote the official version of mis-information when his local Ohio newspaper ran a biographical article about him on 6th August 1944 and coincidentally in that same issue also ran an article concerning Exercise "Tiger" where "*130 soldiers were killed and 312 missing in action*".

MURDOCK however slipped up when interviewed on 16th August 1944 by the Office of Naval Records and Library when he confirmed that infantry were aboard his LST 507. Something that was later hotly denied by the U.S. archives, confirmed by U.S. Army loading sheets and yet no casualties recorded.

ECKSTAM generated interest in Exercise "Tiger" after the war during his retirement and became a focal point for researchers, freely offering information to any enquirer which always supported the official version of events and discouraging new lines of enquiry.

Exhumation

THREE young English WRENS quietly chatted among themselves, huddled together on hard, wooden utility chairs in a room that served as their duty room in a drab hotel requisitioned near the Royal Navy dockyard, Plymouth.

In the middle of the room at a desk sat an elderly male civilian who busied himself taking forms and papers from one tray, reading them, occasionally scribbling on some passing them over his centrally placed bakelite telephone and dropping them in another tray on the opposite end of his desk.

He didn't really approve of these young girls doing a "man's job" of driving cars and lorries but grudgingly accepted that with all young men conscripted into the armed forces, someone had to do this job, but why young girls !

When the telephone rang the WRENS conversation immediately stopped and they all turned to look at the man who picked up the telephone. All they could hear was his side of the conversation as he slowly spoke "*Yes, yes, yes, I understand*".

Replacing the telephone he looked up and said "*Three lorries in one hour, you'll be met in the yard by a motorbike rider who'll take you to your destination and this is secret, so don't talk about it to anyone*".

Shaking his head in exasperation he thought, how could you use young girls on such an important job, and secret too. Still tutting he started filling in the appropriate form for this job, handing a copy to the girls as they left the room.

Right on time a Navy motorcycle rider swept into the yard, stopped his machine, pulled it back on the stand and taking off his gauntlets walked to the three waiting WRENS. "*This is top secret, don't talk about it or anything you might see, you'll follow me and we won't be using the main roads around Kingsbridge as the Yanks' heavy lorries are on them – come on*".

Returning to his motorcycle he kicked it into life, looked over his shoulder and led the three trucks out of the yard and out of Plymouth. All the WRENS had driven throughout south Devon for several months so knew the area well even with all road signposts removed and soon realised they were being led in a roundabout route along lanes in the direction of Dartmouth.

Finally, at 11:00 a.m. the rider halted at the side of the road and signalled the trucks to pull onto the grass verge behind him and then everyone waited. Looking around from their elevated position the WRENS could see reed beds in the distance below them with the sea beyond. Knowing the area well, all recognised they were overlooking Slapton Sands and on the edge of the American battle area.

The young WREN in the first truck had a good view of a field gateway a few yards ahead and noted it was well worn with tyre marks, then on the opposite grass verge next to the open field gate she saw about forty wooden cases stacked in two rows one on top of the other with more boxes being brought from the field all the time.

Thoroughly bored with all the waiting she reached across the cab to unwrap her sandwiches on the seat next to her and sitting up to bite into an unappetising corned beef sandwich she noticed a civilian truck coming towards her from the Dartmouth direction.

She knew some civilian traffic with special passes was allowed to travel along the exercise area perimeter road and watched as it slowed by the field entrance until it was urgently waved on by an American sentry.

Three men in the cab had only briefly looked into the field but saw a bulldozer digging large pits with wooden boxes perched on top of the spoil heaps and six-wheel trucks backed up near the pits. Having been waved on the three discussed what they had seen for only a few moments before reverting to the more popular discussion of football.

Every few minutes a large American truck would appear from the opposite direction and park in front of the boxes obscuring her view until it reversed into the field gateway and drove off the way it had come, back towards Torcross and the main road to Kingsbridge.

Every time this happened she could see the stack of boxes had diminished and this routine went on several times until 2:30 p.m. when the motor cycle rider had a brief conversation on his radio then walked back to the WRENS still sitting in their cabs as they had been instructed and told them their mission had been cancelled and to follow him back to Plymouth.

Taking another circuitous route along the narrow lanes he led the three Royal Navy lorries in the general direction of Dartmouth before joining the main road for Plymouth, again avoiding the town of Kingsbridge.

There the railway station was shut down and guarded by American military police for three days to load three funeral trains with bodies of American casualties in wooden boxes, and only the station master was allowed to be present.

With so many U.S. personnel based in the south west of England and inevitable fatal casualties from accidents, live-fire exercises, illness and natural causes a dedicated rail service operated from Devonport, Plymouth, to transport bodies directly to the American cemetery at Brookwood, Surrey.

A young apprentice working for Southern Railways who operated this service was called to Stonehouse Pool, Devonport dockyard on a minor repair for the signalman Reg Bragg. After the customary mug of tea Reg took the apprentice to a line of five or six stationary goods wagons outside his signal box. "*This is one of several trains*" he said pulling back the sliding door on one wagon and to the young apprentice's horror he saw it contained twenty-five or thirty bodies of American soldiers stacked in layers on wooden cots. To him they appeared to be embalmed and each wore a new khaki uniform with black ties and he knew they were infantry by their lapel badges as some were stationed in his home village.

To Europe

IT is a monumental logistical task to dis-inter bodies from England and transport them to Europe. It is certainly an impossible undertaking without the consent and support of the highest authority at a time when the shipping of essential, tactical supplies and personnel to the European campaign was taking the utmost priority.

But the U.S. Army thought nothing of dis-interring bodies and moving them from one cemetery to another. In Ireland many bodies were moved from civilian cemeteries to official military cemeteries, only to be moved again to mainland Britain or repatriated to the United States.

By August 1944 the Allied campaign in Europe was going well. Paris had been liberated, amphibious landings made in the south of France were rapidly pushing northwards, the Italian campaign was slowly gaining ground and Russia maintained pressure on the Germans' Eastern Front with some spectacular advances. Overall it was an optimistic outlook and a certainty that Allied forces would prevail, giving rise to a confidence that it was an ideal and convenient time to execute the most deceitful part of the Exercise Tiger cover up.

Timing for this operation was vital as American bodies buried in the Devon fields had to be removed before displaced citizens of the Slapton Battle Exercise area were allowed to return to their homes and farms as agreed by September 1944.

This movement of hundreds of bodies at this time shows just how important the cover up was regarded to remove evidence of a disaster far greater than has ever been admitted and witnesses corroborate that is exactly what was done.

Some of the exhumed bodies' journey to Europe was witnessed by John CULLEN, a crew member of Royal Navy Motor Launch 532 based in Cherbourg after the port's liberation in late June 1944 when he was ... "*ordered to escort a large sea going tug from New Orleans. She was towing a "Rhino" and built on the deck of the "Rhino" was a large timber structure approximately 150 ft long by 10 ft high. The skipper of the tug explained the structure. It apparently, contained the bodies of 2500 American Service Men killed in action*". Cherbourg wasn't liberated until late June 1944 and repatriation of combat casualties from European cemeteries to the United States was not started until 1948 so CULLEN's statement of 1944 confirms transportation of American bodies to Normandy although the total number may have been exaggerated by the tug captain.

The destination of bodies in Normandy has already been indicated by official burial records of Robert P. Motley and Donald S. Bryant. Both are confirmed casualties of Exercise "Tiger" and are two cases where the truth has been inadvertently exposed through honest or mistaken administration and indicates a cover-up where other bodies are also buried in France, particularly casualties from 1st and 2nd Battalions, 8th Infantry Regiment who were victims of the beach bombardment disaster on 27th April 1944.

In August 1944 drivers of the 146th QM Truck Company, who had taken bodies from Portland to Brookwood cemetery, were now told they would be transporting the army payroll from England to Normandy.

The twenty eight trucks and drivers selected were sent to Southampton where they were joined by twenty eight military policemen and twenty nine officers who would ride with the convoy.

They all spent a sleepless and nervous night camped in Marshalling Area C-18 on a hillside overlooking Southampton watching "buzz bombs" coming in over the coast every ten minutes and heading inland.

The next afternoon all the "payroll" trucks with Fred Cox "*backed on the LST (were) put on the elevator which took us up to the top deck and we anchored down, then they brought on tanks down in the hold, closed the doors and we left the shore and went out in the dark*".

Two days later a dozen American military police stood in groups of three or four on "Utah" beach at evening high tide peering through the darkness to catch sight of a grey LST slowly approaching them. They had been put on alert only a few hours before to meet this ship when it beached and ordered to ensure it was unloaded swiftly and to keep personnel well away from the unloading.

The ship was to be deliberately run aground as was normal procedure for LSTs to unload their cargo then re-load with casualties and wait for the next high tide to lift them off the beach and re-float them.

The vessel they were expecting was first spotted only a few hundred yards away slowly closing on the beach growing in size until it towered over the waiting soldiers, the bows rose up and ground to a halt pushing a wave of sand and seawater up the beach causing the soldiers to take several backward steps.

Within minutes straining cables and chains creaked and screamed as the huge bow doors split apart until they stood wide open before the internal ramp was slowly lowered, crashing the last few feet into wet sand.

Almost immediately the sound of heavy engines echoed in the dark bowels of the ship, growing louder until a line of tanks appeared at the top of the ramp, each pausing for a few seconds while the driver acclimatised his eyes to the darkness and ensuring he was in the correct position before roaring down the ramp and onto the beach.

The military police watched from either side of the ramp as the tanks were followed by a line of twenty eight trucks which debarked and without pausing crossed the beach, through the cut in the dunes and headed for the causeway leading inland towards Ste Mere Eglise.

Each truck had the canvas hood over the cargo hold with rear curtains drawn tight and an officer and a military policeman in each cab with the driver.

Within minutes the entire convoy of twenty eight trucks of the 146th Quartermaster Truck Company had disappeared into the dark Normandy countryside. The MP's job was over and they sauntered up the beach in groups swapping ribald suggestions as to what was so important about that particular convoy that needed an officer and a military policeman in each truck.

Normandy burials

ON 24th June 1944 all graves registration companies in Normandy were relieved from attachment to the Engineer Special Brigades, reverting to First U.S. Army control.

That same day outside Ste Mere Eglise, Normandy, just after dawn a small dust-covered convoy of trucks, trailers and jeeps carrying the 4th Platoon of 607th Quartermaster Graves Registration Company pulled into a large field surrounded by a thick hedgerow and tall trees. They had been ordered here to establish a new temporary cemetery – Ste Mere Eglise #2.

Originally scheduled to arrive in Normandy on 29th June with Headquarters Platoon they had been quickly attached to the 1st Engineer Special Brigade on 10th May 1944 for the invasion of Utah beach in Normandy to replace the First Platoon which had taken part in Exercise Tiger and was virtually wiped out losing 16 of their 24 men.

Already parked alongside the far hedgerow were vehicles of the 603rd QM Graves Registration Company, some of their personnel already spread across the field, busy with long tape measures, banging in tent pegs to mark out the cemetery plots.

A group of unkempt German prisoners of war with dirty field grey uniforms stood beside one of the trucks casually watched by an armed American soldier. Their job was simply to dig graves and manhandle bodies from incoming trucks onto the ground for the graves registration to identify the corpse, remove personal effects and complete their paperwork. Once that was done the prisoners would carry the body to the allocated grave and bury it. Most were happy to do this work and to be out of the fight because now they were fed properly, slept under cover and their welfare protected. All had done their duty to some degree for their fatherland and reached the point in conflict where self-interest took priority and to surrender and survive was the preferred option.

A shout from across the field set them running in that direction and after being given a few directions began to dig into the earth with long handled shovels to create the first graves.

While some 603rd personnel directed their prisoners and others continued marking out the cemetery plots, the 607th climbed out of their vehicles and walked across to other 603rd soldiers setting up their tents.

"*Where've you come from ?*" enquired one. "*'Bout half a mile over there*" was the reply with a wave of the arm in a southerly direction. "*Well we've been drivin' half the night to get here, didn't expect to see anyone else already here*".

The usual soldier exchange of information and rumours followed and soon a working relationship was established with cemetery tasks allocated and coffee on the boil.

This relative inactivity didn't last long as truck after truck intermittently arrived over the next six weeks carrying bodies fresh from combat for the routine process of identification and burial.

Despite this pressure of constant daily deliveries the 607th intermittently returned to the emergency burial grounds at Hiesville,

St Martin and 607 Macon to exhume those bodies and return them to Ste Mere Eglise #2.

Eventually the number of bodies brought to this cemetery eased off until one dawn in late August when a seemingly never-ending line of 6x6 trucks pulled into the field.

This was a curious convoy as all trucks had their cargo area covered with canvas tilts. Usually bodies arrived in open backed trucks or trailers which made it easier to move around the bodies to load and unload them.

Some German prisoners were sent back from grave digging to unload the bodies and when they crowded round the tail of the first truck were surprised to see not mangled, bloody corpses covered in blankets, mattress covers or parachutes, but wooden boxes.

A few quizzical glances were exchanged between the Americans as they gathered round the first truck and saw the boxes then a sergeant shouted to the driver "*What's this?*"

"*Twelve bodies for you. We've all got the same*" pointing down the line of twenty eight trucks. "*Here*" he said "*Here's the manifest*" handing a crumpled sheet to the sergeant "*We'll give you a hand to unload*".

Looking down the line of trucks and mentally assessing the enormous task the sergeant quickly accepted the offer.

This was extremely unusual to receive bodies in wooden caskets but the paperwork in every instance was completed satisfactorily making the task of interment much easier and quicker, in fact by noon every casket had been buried and the convoy had left the field.

Emergency cemeteries

AS AMERICAN troops pressed west from "Utah" beach towards the town of Saint Lo to cut off the Cotentin peninsula with a simultaneous strike northwards to secure the port of Cherbourg at the northern tip of the peninsula they encountered the infamous "Bocage". This medieval chequer board of small fields each enclosed by a deep earth bank surmounted by almost impenetrable, thorny hedging was ideal for defence and exploited to the full by the hard pressed Germans who inflicted grievous casualties upon the attacking American infantry.

The alarming and unexpected number of fatal casualties suffered by the Americans during this campaign known as the "Battle of the hedgerows" was an influencing factor to open another temporary cemetery – Ste Mere Eglise #2 (3586) as it was estimated if casualties continued at that current rate then Ste Mere Eglise #1 (3584) which had been burying bodies since 9th June simply wouldn't have the space to bury them all.

Despite this growing number of casualties the Allied beachhead in Normandy was firmly established by the end of June 1944. The port of Cherbourg had been taken by 25th June and military organisation and administration began to get a grip of the campaign, including the disposition of casualties.

Throughout Normandy burials to date had been made in an almost haphazard fashion with some bodies buried where they fell or taken to the nearest official temporary cemetery regardless of what unit they were from. Just over two weeks after D-Day when Ste Mere Eglise #2 (3586) cemetery opened it was officially dedicated as the resting place for VII Corps casualties. VII Corps was the overseeing organisation for all units that made the initial landings on "Utah" beach, including the 8th Infantry Regiment and 1st Engineer Special Brigade both of which had participated in Exercise "Tiger".

Just outside the hamlet of Blosville south of Ste Mere Eglise situated in the centre of American airborne drops was probably the first temporary cemetery opened in Normandy on 7th June 1944. Initially to accommodate fifty casualties of the American air drop from the immediate vicinity, the small graves registration crew were swamped as casualties poured in and only two days later there were hundreds of American and German bodies awaiting burial. Local French volunteers were enlisted and German prisoners of war diverted from PoW enclosures to cope with an increasing number of bodies to be buried but they were almost overwhelmed by the daily influx.

"607 Macon" was established as a matter of urgently burying dead of the first few hours of the invasion at Utah beach and was created by the 607th QM Graves Registration Company adding the name of the commanding general of the 83rd Infantry Division Robert C. MACON. Situated alongside the flooded causeway leading from Utah beach to Ste Marie du Mont, within a few days it filled with 190 burials but was soon superseded as the campaign rapidly moved inland.

8th Infantry Regiment had one 6th June casualty buried inland at Blosville, and another curiously buried at St. Laurent behind Omaha beach. This latter burial is unlikely to be correct as the two beachheads were separated by enemy forces until 12th June and tidal flow would not have carried a body eastwards from Utah onto Omaha.

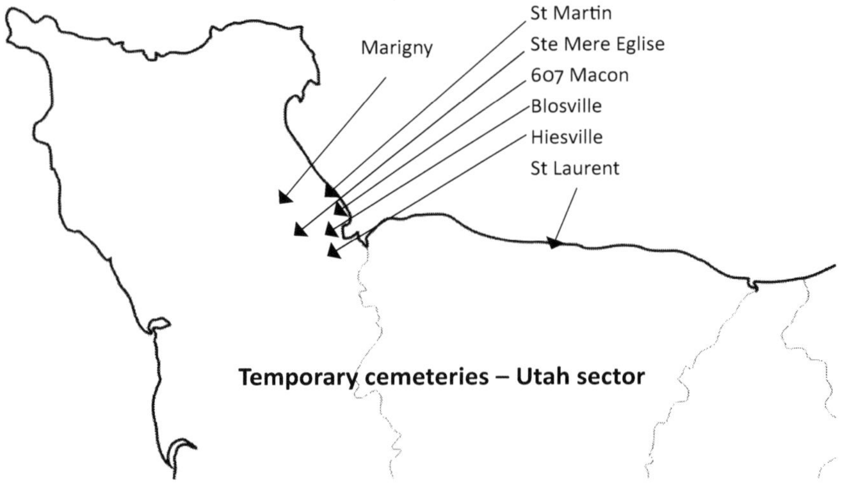

Temporary cemeteries – Utah sector

The official U.S. military history of Operation "Overlord" which details the D-Day landings and subsequent operations marvelled at the light casualties of the "Utah" beach landings stating casualties for the 8th and 22nd Infantry Regiments on D-Day, 6th June 1944 totalled just 12 killed from both regiments.

Other official records (ABMC and NARA) differ putting the total at 32, of which 8 are from 22nd Infantry Regiment and 24 from the 8th Infantry Regiment. If the official U.S. military history is correct, then 20 casualties from these two regiments didn't die on D-Day at all.

The total number of 4th Infantry Division fatalities on 6th June during the "Utah" landings officially varies between 197 and 210 and most of these were from 42nd Field Artillery Battalion when their ship hit a mine and sank before they landed.

According to the 531st Engineer Shore Regiment's official history 18 of their personnel were loaded onto LST 531 for Exercise Tiger and all became fatal casualties although according to U.S. Army loading sheets there were 24 personnel loaded, not 18, leaving 6 casualties unaccounted for.

Of their casualties of 6th June on "Utah" beach totalling another 18, only 7 are acknowledged by the official history as being killed on that date. Of that total, 1 was buried at Brookwood, England, where Exercise Tiger casualties were initially buried, 1 at Blosville, 12 at 607 Macon, and the initial burial sites of the remaining 4 have never been identified although their names appear weeks later as being buried at Ste Mere Eglise #2 (3586).

So far cross-checking official records there are 11 casualties from the 531st Engineer Shore Regiment and 20 casualties of 8th Infantry Regiment listed as dying on D-Day, but didn't. This strengthens the case for more "D-Day casualties" of both units having a false date of death having truly perished during Exercise "Tiger".

249 American bodies were moved from Hiesville on 5th July 1944 to Ste Mere Eglise #2. From the early hours of D-Day the chateau at Hiesville had been used as a makeshift aid station for paratroopers, casualties being buried in the chateau grounds.

St Martin de Varreville was also principally for paratrooper casualties in the vicinity of Ste Mere Eglise and their bodies removed to Ste Mere Eglise #2 in August 1944.

Morning Reports

THESE documents are prepared by every U.S. Army company, each day to show the unit's location, number of personnel present for ration purposes together with any changes to their personnel whether hospitalised, wounded, injured, died, joined the unit, transferred or promoted.

With the 8th Infantry Regiment refined as the focus of interest it would be expected their morning reports to show casualties of Exercise Tiger proving that unit suffered fatal casualties during the exercise.

But relevant dates of 27th, 28th and 29th April 1944 for Companies A to H inclusive, are blank. They are completely devoid of routine detail or casualties in stark contrast to Morning Reports of other units involved in Exercise "Tiger" which detail fatal casualties, wounded and missing, movements from home station and in some cases dates they loaded onto specific naval ships.

For the same companies from 6th to 15th June 1944, there are no details of any casualties at all, and for the dates 6th to 9th June 1944 entries exclusively refer to the headquarters units of those companies which were still in Bournemouth, England as the "residue" while the bulk of their units were fighting and dying in Normandy. Morning Reports after 9th June 1944 don't retrospectively show casualties for this period so there is a suspicious blank time slot when casualties weren't recorded at the most basic level. This of course allows manipulation of death dates at the level above – cemetery records.

This lack of detail is in complete contrast to Morning Reports of the 12th Infantry Regiment who landed alongside the 8th Infantry Regiment in Exercise Tiger and on Utah beach on D-Day. Their residue, just like the 8th Infantry Regiment was at Bournemouth,

England for the first few days of the Normandy landings but the 12th do record their casualties in Normandy.

This comparative lack of detail confirms the 8th Infantry Regiment Morning Reports have been deliberately re-written to avoid showing their casualties of Exercise "Tiger".

One outstanding example is Company "G" Morning Reports which have all been signed by Captain James HALEY the company commander on reports dated 27th, 28th and 29th April 1944 – all of them blank. This man was on Slapton beach on those dates and is credited with calling off the Royal Navy beach bombardment but nowhere on these reports is there even a mention of taking part in an exercise.

Other company morning reports of 8th Infantry Regiment are also signed by their company commanders who were also committed with Exercise Tiger and are equally devoid of detail. This again is in stark contrast to other participating units who include every detail of the exercise.

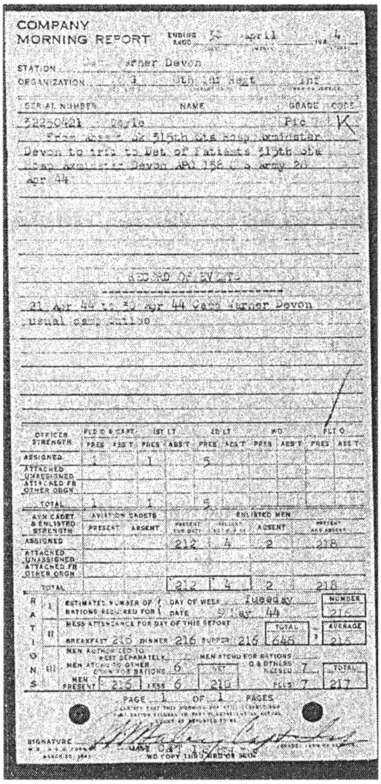
COMPANY
MORNING REPORT ENDING April
STATION Devon
ORGANIZATION
SERIAL NUMBER NAME GRADE CODE
Pfc K
RECORD OF EVENTS
21 Apr 44 Devon

OFFICER STRENGTH	FLD O & CAPT. PRES	FLD O & CAPT. ABS'T	1ST LT PRES	1ST LT ABS'T	2D LT PRES	2D LT ABS'T	WO PRES	WO ABS'T	FLT O PRES	FLT O ABS'T
ASSIGNED	1		1		5					
ATTACHED UNASSIGNED										
ATTACHED FR OTHER ORGN										
TOTAL	1		1		5					

AVN CADET & ENLISTED STRENGTH	AVIATION CADETS PRESENT	AVIATION CADETS ABSENT	ENLISTED MEN PRESENT FOR DUTY	ENLISTED MEN PRESENT	ENLISTED MEN ABSENT	ENLISTED MEN PRESENT AND ABSENT
ASSIGNED			212	4	2	218
ATTACHED UNASSIGNED						
ATTACHED FR OTHER ORGN						
TOTAL			212	4	2	218

RATIONS
I ESTIMATED NUMBER OF RATIONS REQUIRED FOR DAY OF WEEK Tuesday DATE 9 May 44 NUMBER 216
II MESS ATTENDANCE FOR DAY OF THIS REPORT BREAKFAST 216 DINNER 216 SUPPER 216 TOTAL 648 ÷ 3 AVERAGE 216
III MEN AUTHORIZED TO MESS SEPARATELY MEN ATCHD TO OTHER ORGN FOR RATIONS 6 MEN ATCHD FOR RATIONS O & OTHERS MESSED 7
MEN PRESENT 216 LESS 6 NET 210 PLUS 7 TOTAL 217
PAGE 1 OF 1 PAGES
SIGNATURE
WD COPY THRU

The conclusion is that 8th Infantry Regiment Morning Reports for 27/28/29 April 1944 may have been accurately completed but destroyed, re-written and presented to company commanders after Exercise Tiger for signature. Where that was not practical, or company commanders were absent, they were signed by the Regimental Personnel Officer 1st Lieutenant W. E. HOLLIS or Chief Warrant Officer Lawrence E. KNECHT, his deputy. For the dates 6th to 9th June most have been signed by HOLLIS or by KNECHT who it is certain were both still in England at that time.

The entry for G Company, 8th Infantry Regiment on 30th April Morning Report reads "*21 Apr 44 to 30 Apr 44 camp Warner Devon Usual camp duties*", and the personnel summary shows the entire company present at Camp Warner when in fact they were still in the Slapton hinterland.

The morning report of 10th June 1944 for Company A shows Maurice C. LAWSON was killed in France on 6th June 1944 which is correct. It also shows Pfc Richard ANTOSZEWSKI, whom the American Battle Monuments Commission state was missing in action on 8th July 1944 was in fact dropped from the regimental rolls on 6th June 1944 indicating he was killed or missing on that date, or even on 27th April.

Pfc Clarence G. LEQUE was also "dropped from rolls" on 6th June 1944 and was in fact Missing in Action on that date. His parents were advised in December 1944 that he was missing and later informed he had died of wounds on 6th June 1944.

Pfc Robert COVINGTON is shown with LEQUE as "dropped from rolls" on the same date suggesting he was also missing or killed in action but there is no record whatever of COVINGTON on any archive source or any record to confirm his fate.

As other 4th Infantry Division units were able to record their casualties from across the English Channel there is no good reason why the 8th didn't do likewise, except submitting blank versions allowed the versatility of changing death dates from April to June 1944.

Other casualty sources

IF the 8th Infantry Regiment's Morning Reports have been altered, cross checking other sources of casualty listings should identify their casualties.

G-1 daily casualty reports were compiled in Normandy to gauge the strength of the regiment as a fighting unit and it becomes obvious that within a few days of landing on D-Day the regiment incurred casualties at a much faster rate than anticipated as demands for replacements grew stronger by the day.

Cognisant of the fact these reports were compiled under combat conditions the accuracy of casualties cannot be relied upon. While many men reported as "missing" on a particular date may simply have been engaged in combat and not able to report to higher authority of their predicament only to later return safe and well, or they may have become fatal casualties.

Therefore these reports cannot be relied upon for accuracy as their numbers of casualties are at wide variance with other sources on both dates and numbers.

The 8th Infantry Regiment G-1 daily journal however confirms the regiment's "residue" including the Adjutant General's unit with HOLLIS and KNECHT remained in England and did not arrive in Normandy until approximately 10th June 1944.

In 1947 the ABMC published their list of 8th Infantry Regiment casualties compiled from their own data and while it appears almost complete it does contain errors of name spelling and inaccurate service numbers either through faulty transcription or original mistake.

Burial reports

PREPARED by Quartermaster Graves Registration Service these are weekly consolidated lists of "Field reports" compiled by Graves Registration personnel at combat and temporary cemeteries at the time of burial showing a casualty's name, rank, assigned service number, unit, date of burial and grave number. These are not listed in strict sequence of date or location suggesting pressure to rapidly produce them and typed as individual "field reports" arrived regardless of date or location.

These have also had false information fed into them highlighted by Donald S BRYANT. A confirmed casualty of 28th April 1944 during Exercise "Tiger" he was, according to these burial sheets, buried at 607 Macon on 8th June 1944 and re-interred in Ste Mere Eglise #2 on 25th June 1944. Repatriated to the United States in 1948 his headstone within Long Island National Cemetery shows his date of death as 6th June 1944.

This is a classic example of the method used to minimise Exercise Tiger casualties by shifting the true date of death in April 1944 to a fictitious one within the Normandy campaign.

This administrative chicanery takes more twists as Staff Sergeant Edward T CARRIKER, according to the 8th Infantry Regiment Morning Report was wounded on 6th June 1944 yet according to the burial report he was buried at sea on 15 July 1944 and recorded today by ABMC as Missing in action.

Some were even buried before their date of death according to these burial reports when compared with other sources. Private Michael J NOLAN, 8th Infantry Regiment died on 25th August 1944 yet according to burial sheets was buried at Ste Mere Eglise #1 on 17th June 1944. His alleged death date in late August coincides with the time period bodies were exhumed from fields above Slapton Sands so he is undoubtedly a casualty of 27th April 1944.

Coxswain James Donald PETERS, U.S. Navy aboard LST 531 was buried at sea on 28th April 1944 according to the burial sheets but Brookwood cemetery have him recorded as being buried there on 3 May 1944 and his body repatriated to Pennsylvania at the end of August 1948.

Technician 5th grade Norbert F SIMON, 8th Infantry Regiment was buried at Ste Mere Eglise on 17th June 1944 but his date of death is 28th June 1944.

From these few examples it is clear these records have been deliberately infiltrated with false details which inevitably casts doubt upon the accuracy of many other burials in the Normandy temporary cemeteries.

One example of the truth slipping out from under the cover up is shown on burial sheet dated 13th August 1944 where four 8th Infantry Regiment casualties, all with an alleged date of death of 24th July 1944 were listed as buried at Cambridge ABMC cemetery.

Private Kenneth P. AUSTIN
Technician Sergeant Carl R. CHAPMAN
2nd Lieutenant Tryon CUTTER
1st Lieutenant William R. DELL

This was quickly corrected two days later on a subsequent burial sheet stating "*Weekly report of burial #98 dated 13 Aug 44 erroneously show the above men buried at Cambridge, request your copy of subject report be changed to comply with this correction*".

These men were buried at Ste Mere Eglise #2, not Cambridge. Again the date of these burial reports coincide with the time period bodies were being exhumed from the Devon fields and transported to Normandy.

Many casualties of the first few days of the D-Day operation are not shown on these reports as being buried in any emergency burial ground but appear weeks later buried directly in Ste Mere Eglise #2. The explanation here is that the published death dates are incorrect and the bodies really didn't lie in any temporary cemetery in Normandy but were exhumed from England and buried directly into Ste Mere Eglise #2.

As the grim task of consolidating Normandy combat casualties into large temporary cemeteries, the initial emergency burial grounds were emptied by 4th Platoon, 607th QM Graves Registration Company.

There seems to be an indecent haste to empty 607 Macon into Ste Mere Eglise #2 as most were reburied there as soon as it opened on 24th June 1944. This coincides with a large number of 8th Infantry Regiment casualties all allegedly killed on 24th June and buried there the same day. Whether this is true or their names were simply added to the burial sheets is open to speculation.

607th Graves Registration personnel tasked with running Ste Mere Eglise #2 were hard pressed to keep pace with the daily arrival of bodies for burial despite increasing their workforce of French locals and German prisoners of war.

Despite the pressure at this cemetery there are just too many inconsistencies to be attributed to sloppy record keeping as Graves Registration units prided themselves upon accuracy and thoroughness despite often operating under difficult conditions.

Anomalies here include "double burials" where soldiers from different units with differing dates of death are buried in the same grave at Ste Mere Eglise #2 suggesting one or both were not buried at all and their grave numbers were used merely as administrative conveniences as part of the documentary deception.

Double burials:-

ANDERSON Howard	3878 QM Gas Supply Co	died 6 July
buried 6 July	3586	C-6-110
CAROTHERS Earlie	364 Eng Gen Svc Regt	died 7 July
buried 7 July	3586	C-6-110
BACHAREK Joseph A	60 Inf Regt 90 Div	died 13 July
buried 13 July	3586	O-6-115
BORTH Ronald R	359 Inf Regt 90 Div	died 3 July
buried 19 July	3586	O-6-115
BAKER Clifford E	3041 Gr Reg Co	died 13June
buried 27 June	3586	B-9-164
* initially buried 607 Macon 13 June		
PARKER James G	22 Inf Regt 4 Div	died 23June
buried 29 June	3586	B-9-164
* burial sheet states 12 Inf Regt 4 Div		

BOWLING Charles B	313 Inf Regt 79 Div	died24 June
buried 28 June	3586	C-8-157
NORRIS Willis E	331 Inf Regt 83 Div	died 5 July
buried 8 July	3586	C-8-157
CRUMRINE Richard R	47 Inf Regt 9 Div	died 13 July
buried 14 July	3586	O-4-79
PAGE Robert K	2 Ranger Bn	died 22 July
buried 23 July	3586	O-4-79
SHAHAN Lewis J	39 Inf Regt 9 Div	died 17 July
buried 17 July	3586	O-1-19
WEGEHAUPT Karl W	957 FA Bn	died 25 July
buried 25 July	3586	O-1-19
VOLLER William J	8 Inf Regt 4 Div	died 22June
buried 24 June	3586	D-1-13
FOX William J	5 Ranger Bn	died 6 June
buried unknown	D-1-13	

Many are shown on the ABMC "*U.S. Rosters of wartime casualties*" as being initially buried at 3586 which is not always corroborated by burial sheets, suggesting they were never buried there at all and ABMC records have been corrupted by incorrect information on official source documents.

Nathan J DEVILLIER is recorded on the U.S. Rosters of WW2 dead as buried at Ste Mere Eglise #1 yet on burial sheets he is shown as being buried at La Cambe.

Charles E METZ died on 28th April 1944 as a member of the 70 Tank Battalion but records show he was in 35 Signal Construction Battalion. Both units participated in Exercise Tiger.

One clumsy attempt to minimise casualties of the 8th Infantry Regiment was to change their unit despite confirmed membership within other documents.

BERTONCELLO John J	8 Inf Regt	to 156 Inf Regt
BEYO Paul A -	4th Inf Div	to 60 Inf Regt 9 Div
BLACKWELL Robert V	8 Inf Regt	to 60 Inf Regt 9 Div
BOBACK Michael J	8 Inf Regt	to 26 Inf Regt
BRADSHAW Carl A	8 Inf Regt	to 9 Inf Regt
CAMP Robert H -	8 Inf Regt	to 175 Inf Regt 29 Div

DEHNE George C	8 Inf Regt	to MP Platoon, 4 Inf Div
EDMONDS Clarence G	8 Inf Regt	to 22 Inf Regt
EVERSMAN Corneluis H	8 Inf Regt	to 708 Ord L M Co
HAACK Herman -	8 Inf Regt	to 354 Inf Regt
HENSLEY Harvey S	8 Inf Regt	to 217 Repl Co
HOLTON William A	8 Inf Regt	to 8 Inf Div
INCH George W -	8 Inf Regt	to 113 Inf Regt
* Date of death 27th April 1944 buried at Marigny		
ISTELL Erwin M -	8 Inf Regt	to 329 Inf Regt
MILLER Harry W	8 Inf Regt	to 286 JASCO
MILLER James H -	8 Inf Regt	to 302 Inf Regt
* buried 5 July, died 2 August 1944		
MURPHY Ray T -	8 Inf Regt	to 314 Inf Regt
MUSS Henry -	8 Inf Regt	to 60 Inf Regt 9 Div
PETRILLO Joseph S	8 Inf Regt	to 358 Inf Regt
SWANSON John B	8 Inf Regt	to 4 Div Arty
WALL Carter W -	8 Inf Regt	to 286 JASCO

The outstanding casualty in this list is George W. Inch. Killed on the first day of Exercise Tiger yet buried in Normandy on 31st July 1944 and when reburied at Arlington cemetery given a date of death as 27th July 1944 instead of 27th April 1944.

Remembrance

IN the pouring rain the old man's fingers moved slowly along the name "*Gearhart Walter F*" etched on the wall of the missing at Cambridge cemetery, tracing each letter of his best buddy in the 625th Ordnance Ammunition Company all those years ago.

There were only two survivors of his unit from Exercise "Tiger" and this one was fulfilling his wartime promise to return to England.

Reaching the end of the name his hand fell to his side and oblivious to the falling rain his head dropped, mouth tightened and tears welled up uncontrollably as he recalled their shared wartime years.

Most vividly he recalled Wally's romance with a young British WREN, Gwen Marshall, who was also stationed at Falmouth, Cornwall, and the sheer joy of Wally each time he received one of her letters. She and Wally planned to marry at the war's end and move back to Ohio which already had the blessing of his family.

They were both used to each other being out of touch for operational reasons but the cruellest blow fell upon Gwen when her last letter was returned to her with the word "missing" handwritten on the envelope.

She could find no news of Wally and towards the end of May 1944 even the Red Cross were unable to help, simply stating "*at present his name does not appear on any prisoner of war or casualty list*" but she continued to search for Wally hoping, just hoping, he was alive.

But by 13th April 1945 she had her answer. The U.S. Army Casualty Division replied to her enquiry that "Cpl Gearhart was killed in action in the English Channel on 28 April 1944".

Conclusion

THERE was a masterful cover up to conceal the true number of casualties of Exercise Tiger that succeeded for over sixty years.

It was conceived and executed by U.S. Navy Commander Virgil Eben Korns with the approval and blessing of the highest military command in Europe.

With precision he covered every eventuality but what he did not include in his calculations of documentary deceit was the honesty and dedication to accuracy of lowly service personnel and civilian clerks tasked with recording deaths in combat. There is no doubt they were ordered to insert false information as they typed up the burial sheets but through honesty, mistake or lack of checking, clues were there all the time.

Just two such instances have enabled the corner of his shameful deception to be lifted to reveal more cases and expose the entire cover up. The blatant mis-use of Ste Mere Eglise #2 temporary cemetery as a burial destination is shown to be a documentary convenience simply because alleged dates of death and burial do not match conventional and true situations.

In many cases this is highlighted where no interim burial record exists between death and interment which is a necessary element to preserve the written chain of burials.

Dead soldiers of 8th Infantry Regiment recorded in this manner were victims of the Royal Navy's beach bombardment on 27th April 1944 at Slapton Sands and those double loaded onto the doomed LST 507.

Many of these bodies were exhumed and moved to Normandy, but some still lie beneath those green fields.

Utah beach casualties on D-Day were so light it compelled the cover up to spread the "extra 300" Exercise Tiger casualties throughout the Normandy campaign, not just 6th June 1944, D-Day.

So many examples of wrong or incorrect detail are shown on burial sheets and ABMC records that question their veracity. Developing this distrust further in the burial chain of events raises the unthinkable that there are some empty graves in Normandy and their named occupants are still buried in forgotten mass graves in England.

Epilogue:

ON August 19th, 1945 the New York Herald Tribune carried a United Press report from Dartmouth, England. "*A stained glass window in the north wall of the chapel of the Royal Naval College here, known as the St. Columba (*patron saint of seafarers*) window, is a permanent symbol of the uniting of the British and American Navies for the invasion of Europe. The window was presented to the college by members of the United States Navy assigned to duty here when this base was established as one of the British ports for United States Navy invasion operations. It was recently unveiled and dedicated in a special service in the chapel. Commodore V. E. Korns commander of the amphibious base, United Kingdom, United States Navy, made the formal presentation. He said the window was a token of the appreciation of the men who had been stationed here and should remain as a token of the good will between the British and American Navies and people*".